The Civil War: Essential Histories

The Civil War

Bull Run and Other Eastern Battles
1861–May 1863

Robert O'Neill, Series Editor; and Gary W. Gallagher

ROSEN
PUBLISHING
New York

This edition published in 2011 by:

The Rosen Publishing Group, Inc.
29 East 21st Street
New York, NY 10010

Additional end matter copyright © 2011 by The Rosen Publishing Group, Inc.

Library of Congress Cataloging-in-Publication Data

O'Neill, Robert John.
The Civil War: Bull Run and other Eastern battles 1861–May 1863 / Robert O'Neill, Gary W. Gallagher.
    p. cm.—(The Civil War: Essential histories)
Includes bibliographical references and index.
ISBN 978-1-4488-0387-3 (library binding)
1. United States—History—Civil War, 1861–1865—Campaigns—Juvenile literature. 2. East (U.S.)—History, Military—19th century—Juvenile literature. 3. United States—Politics and government—1861–1865—Juvenile literature. I. Gallagher, Gary W. II. Title.
E470.2.O54 2011
973.7'31—dc22

    2010006103

Manufactured in the United States of America

CPSIA Compliance Information: Batch #S10YA: For further information, contact Rosen Publishing, New York, New York, at 1-800-237-9932.

Copyright © 2001 Osprey Publishing Limited. First published in paperback by Osprey Publishing Limited.

On the cover: Sumter Light Guards of Americus, Georgia. (Library of Congress)

Contents

Introduction

The Civil War towers over the landscape of United States history. The young American republic had experienced tensions with France and a second war with Great Britain in the decades following ratification of the Constitution, but no foreign power had posed a serious threat to its viability as a nation. Such a threat came from within in 1860, when the presidential election initiated a political crisis that saw 11 slaveholding states band together to form the Confederate States of America. Fierce political disagreement gave way to war in April 1861, as Confederates insisted on their right to leave the Union and the North refused to allow them to go. No one anticipated the scale of military fury and social disruption that ensued. Four years of brutal fighting claimed more than a million military casualties, sucked hundreds of thousands of civilians into its vortex, and liberated four million enslaved African Americans. The social and economic system based on chattel slavery that the seceding states had sought to protect lay in ruins. The inviolability of the Union had been confirmed, as had the supremacy of the national government over the individual states. In the longer term, preservation of the Union made possible the modern American colossus, which figured so prominently in twentieth-century history.

The generation that experienced the war struggled to understand its scope and consequences. In his second inaugural address, delivered on 4 March 1865, Abraham Lincoln spoke of the "great contest which still absorbs the attention, and engrosses the energies of the nation." The President affirmed that "neither party expected for the war, the magnitude, or the duration, which it has already attained." Turning his attention to slavery, Lincoln added that neither side "anticipated that the *cause* of the conflict might cease with, or even before, the contest itself should cease. Each looked for an easier triumph, and a result less fundamental and astounding." Poet Walt Whitman found in the war's result an affirmation of the essential bond among all Americans. He viewed the conflict "not as a struggle of two distinct and separate peoples, but a conflict ... between the passions and paradoxes of one and the same identity—perhaps the only terms on which that identity could really become fused, homogeneous and lasting."

Many unrepentant ex-Confederates would have disagreed with Whitman's emphasis on Americans as one people, preferring to celebrate their failed effort to carve out a distinct destiny. Their arguments became part of the "Lost Cause" interpretation of the war and proved remarkably durable. Former Confederate general Jubal A. Early, a leading Lost Cause controversialist, urged white southerners to honour "the graves of our fallen heroes" and "cherish the remembrance of their deeds, and see that justice is done to their memories." Early insisted that the Confederate experiment had been noble and hoped his old comrades would hold dear "the holy memories connected with our glorious though unsuccessful struggle."

Americans have been fascinated by the Civil War to a degree unequalled by interest in any other aspect of their national history. Many are drawn by the sheer size of the conflict, which dwarfs all other American wars in terms of percentage of population physically affected in a significant way. They also seek to understand the paramount issues that divided mid-nineteenth-century Americans—preservation of the Union versus state rights, freedom or slavery for millions of black people, and the definition of the relationship between state and central authority. At no other time in United States history has more been at stake. The fact that it was a homegrown affair, a gigantic contest between Americans on their own soil, also appeals to modern readers. Finally, the war brought to the fore a fascinating group of characters, including Lincoln and Robert E. Lee. In one of the war's many ironies, the great rebel leader Lee, rather than Ulysses S. Grant or some other Union war hero, stands alongside Lincoln as one of the conflict's two most popular figures.

The Osprey Essential History Series devotes four volumes to the American Civil War, each of which gives attention to the home fronts and common soldiers as well as to generals and battles. The first explores long-term sectional tensions and the immediate political crises that triggered fighting before moving on to the campaigns and battles in the Eastern Theater between May 1861 and June 1863. The theater embraced Virginia, Maryland and southern Pennsylvania, providing the geographical arena in which the Union's Army of the Potomac and the Confederacy's Army of Northern Virginia fought a series of storied battles. Robert E. Lee, "Stonewall" Jackson and James Longstreet carried southern martial fortunes to their zenith during this period, forging victories at the Seven Days, Second Manassas, Fredericksburg and Chancellorsville. The Army of the Potomac managed just one strategic success, repelling Lee's army at the Battle of Antietam in September 1862. George B. McClellan, who built the northern army into a formidable force but lacked the essential qualities of a great commander, stood out among the Union officers who failed to win a decisive victory in Virginia.

This volume closes with Confederates celebrating their success at Chancellorsville but mourning the death of Jackson. On the Union side, Joseph Hooker led the Army of the Potomac, but inspired little confidence among his soldiers or the northern public. Both civilian populations had come to terms with the prospect of a long and costly war, yearning for peace but expecting more fighting. That grim expectation would be met in ample measure during the final two years of struggle.

Chronology

1820 Missouri Compromise admits Missouri as a slave state, but prohibits slavery elsewhere in the Louisiana territory above latitude 36° 30" N

1831 Nat Turner's slave rebellion sends shock waves through the South; William Lloyd Garrison founds abolitionist newspaper *The Liberator*

1845 Texas admitted to the Union

1846–48 War between the United States and Mexico

1846 Wilmot Proviso calls for barring slavery from lands acquired from Mexico

1848 Free Soil Party fields presidential candidate

1850 Compromise of 1850 includes admission of California as a free state and enactment of a tough Fugitive Slave Law

1852 Whig Party fields its last serious presidential candidate, signals breakdown of the two-party system; publication of Harriet Beecher Stowe's *Uncle Tom's Cabin* makes many northerners sensitive to the issue of slavery

1854 Kansas–Nebraska Act inflames sectional tensions

1857 The Supreme Court's Dred Scott decision opens Federal territories to slavery and outrages many people in the North

1859 John Brown's raid on Harpers Ferry intensifies sectional tensions

1860 **November 6** Abraham Lincoln elected President
December 20 South Carolina secedes from the Union

1861 **January 9–February 1** The remaining six states of the Lower South secede

February 4–March 11 Convention of delegates from the seceded states in Montgomery, Alabama, writes a Constitution and selects Jefferson Davis and Alexander H. Stephens as provisional President and Vice-President of the Confederate States of America

March 4 Lincoln's first inaugural address

April 12–13 Confederate bombardment results in the surrender of Fort Sumter

April 15 Lincoln calls for 75,000 volunteers to suppress the rebellion

April 17–June 8 Four states of the Upper South secede in response to Lincoln's call for volunteers

Early May Winfield Scott briefs President Lincoln about a strategy later known as the "Anaconda Plan"

May 20 Confederate Congress votes to move national government from Montgomery, Alabama, to Richmond, Virginia

July 21 Battle of First Manassas or Bull Run

November 1 George B. McClellan replaces Winfield Scott as General-in-Chief of the US army

1862 **February 25** President Lincoln signs the Legal Tender Act, which creates national Treasury notes soon dubbed "greenbacks"

March 17 George B. McClellan begins movement of Union troops to Virginia Peninsula

April 16 Confederate Congress passes the first National Conscription Act in American history

May 8 "Stonewall" Jackson wins the Battle of McDowell, the first of several victories in his Shenandoah valley campaign; other victories follow at Front Royal (May 23), First Winchester (May 25), Cross Keys (June 8), and Port Republic (June 9)

May 15 US Congress passes the Homestead Bill

May 31–June 1 Battle of Seven Pines or Fair Oaks

June 1 Robert E. Lee takes command of Confederate army at Richmond

June 25–July 1 Seven Days battles reverse a tide of Union military success as Lee drives McClellan away from Richmond in action at Mechanicsville (June 26), Gaines's Mill (June 27), Savage Station (June 29), Glendale or Frayser's Farm (June 30), and Malvern Hill (July 1)

August 9 Battle of Cedar Mountain

August 28–30 Battle of Second Manassas or Bull Run

September 17 Battle of Antietam or Sharpsburg ends Lee's first invasion of the North

September 22 Lincoln issues his preliminary Emancipation Proclamation

November 5 Ambrose E. Burnside replaces McClellan as commander of the Army of the Potomac

December 13 Battle of Fredericksburg

1863 January 1 Lincoln issues final Emancipation Proclamation

January 25 Joseph Hooker replaces Burnside as commander of the Army of the Potomac

February 25 US Congress passes the National Banking Act

March 3 US Congress passes the Enrollment Act, which institutes a national draft

April 2 Women take to the streets in the Richmond "bread riot" to protest against food shortages

April 24 Confederate Congress enacts the Tax-in-Kind Law, a highly unpopular measure requiring agricultural producers to give a portion of various crops to the national government

May 1–4 Battle of Chancellorsville

May 10 "Stonewall" Jackson dies

Sectional tensions divide the United States, 1820–1860

Sectional tensions simmered and periodically erupted into violent controversy in the United States during the four decades preceding the outbreak of war in April 1861. If viewed retrospectively with knowledge of the enormous slaughter of 1861–65 in mind, the years between 1820 and 1860 can appear as a time when Americans watched almost helplessly as their nation drifted towards disaster. Yet most Americans of this period did not wake up every morning eager to focus on the ways in which the North and South differed. They pursued their mundane activities without knowing that a gigantic war lurked in the years ahead. Lacking a sense that time was ticking away for a young republic destined to undergo a trauma of unimagined proportion, they typically concentrated on local or state, rather than national, political issues.

Historians have debated whether the free states of the North and the slaveholding states of the South had developed into significantly different societies by the late 1850s. Some have described two essentially different civilizations divided across a fault line delineated by the institution of slavery. Others point to a common language, a joint history dominated by the revolutionary struggle against Great Britain, and other shared characteristics to insist that differences were minor when compared to commonalities.

Much of this debate fails to emphasize the crucial point that many, and perhaps most, northerners and white southerners *believed* that major differences divided them.

In the four decades before the Civil War, the North moved rapidly towards a more urban society with a powerful manufacturing sector. By 1860, 15 of the nation's 16 largest cities were in states that remained loyal to the Union. George Inness's *The Lackawanna Valley* captures this transformation, with its lone figure gazing across a largely pastoral Pennsylvania landscape towards a puffing locomotive and factories sending spirals of smoke into the air. (National Gallery of Art, Washington, DC)

Northerners looked south and saw a white population profoundly influenced by slavery. Many white southerners, in turn, considered northerners an almost alien people bent on interfering with the slave-based southern society. It makes little difference whether a true gulf separated northern and southern society. If people believed there were differences, they acted accordingly, behaved as if the two sections had developed differently, and thus stood at odds in many ways.

Economic and social developments

Although broad generalizations about the two sections can obscure almost as much as they reveal, some trends in northern and southern development between the establishment of the Constitution and the close of the antebellum (pre-war) period help set up the final sectional crisis. The North's population grew far more rapidly, allowing the free states to gain an increasingly lopsided majority in the national House of Representatives and to win control of Senate in 1850. The North attracted most of the nation's new immigrants, many of whom settled in rapidly growing cities. Far more urban than the slaveholding South (one-quarter of northerners lived in urban areas in 1860, one-tenth of southerners), the North also possessed most of the nation's industrial, commercial and financial strength. Yet a substantial agricultural sector employed roughly 40 percent of the region's workers in 1860. Yeoman farmers with relatively small holdings dominated northern agriculture.

Religion helped shape northern economic and social life. A vibrant form of Yankee Protestantism trumpeted the virtues of hard work and thrift, while warning against abuse of alcohol or excess of any type. This religious strain helped create an environment conducive to capitalist expansion and the creation of an American industrial and commercial colossus. The same Protestant ethic prompted many

Abraham Lincoln in May 1860, just before growing the whiskers he would wear for the rest of his life. He had entered the national stage during the 1858 senatorial race in Illinois. Although he lost that contest to Stephen A. Douglas, a series of debates between the candidates had brought Lincoln to the attention of Republicans across the nation. (Author's collection)

northerners to embrace reform movements that sought to curb drinking, enhance public education, improve conditions in prisons and asylums for the mentally ill and, most importantly in terms of sectional relations, end the institution of slavery. Significant elements of the northern populace resisted the models of reform, purposeful labor and material acquisition—including many Democrats, urban Catholics and residents of the lower sections of the midwestern states who looked south across the Ohio river for many of their economic, familial and social ties. But the North's political and economic leadership tended to subscribe to the Yankee Protestant ethic, thereby setting a standard for the entire section.

By the mid-1850s, the free labor ideology had taken firm root across much of the North. It insisted that labor and capital need not be at odds. According to Whigs and later Republicans who espoused the free labor ideology, every man in the United States (only men could vote, and women occupied a distinctly disadvantaged legal position) possessed almost limitless potential. Poorer men could use their own labor to acquire capital, ascend from the ranks of workers to become property owners, and create a comfortable and rewarding life for themselves and their families. Harsh inequalities of wealth among northerners suggested that this ideal remained far from assured, but political leaders such as Abraham Lincoln, himself a remarkable example of how a poor man could rise, painted a picture of glorious capitalist development. "The prudent, penniless beginner in the world, labors for wages awhile," stated Lincoln in 1859, "saves a surplus with which to buy tools or land, for himself; then labors on his own account another while, and at length hires another new beginner to help him." This was *free labor*—the just and generous, and prosperous system, which opens the way for all—gives hope to all, and energy, and progress, and improvement of condition to all."

Many northerners looked south and saw a land of lazy, cruel, poorly educated, violent people stained by the taint of slavery and opposed to the ideas that would allow the United States to fulfill its capitalist destiny. Because slavery closed opportunities to white working-class men in the South, and degraded them by forcing them to compete with chattels, the free labor ideology could not flourish below the Mason–Dixon Line, which symbolized the division between the free North and the slave South. (In fact, the Mason–Dixon Line formed the boundary between Pennsylvania, a free state, and Maryland, a slave state.) The failure of the free labor ideology to flourish, believed its advocates, in turn compromised the future of the nation.

The South did present a striking contrast in many ways. Steadily losing ground in terms of comparative population, its networks of roads, railroads and canals lagged far behind those of the North. Roughly 80 percent of its population labored in agriculture, and the overwhelming bulk of southern wealth was invested in slaves and land. Wealthy slaveholders dominated the region politically and socially, producing cash crops of cotton, sugar, tobacco and rice. Southern cotton fed northern and European textile mills, as well as contributing enormously to the nation's favorable balance of trade. Cities were fewer and smaller than in the North, white southerners were on average less well educated, and southern religion, though predominantly Protestant as in the North, was more concerned with personal salvation than with reforming or

This painting of a cotton plantation reinforces an image of the antebellum South as a place of vast plantations and powerful slaveholders. Such estates did exist, and their owners wielded enormous economic and political power. But the large majority of white southerners lived on small farms with no slaves. (Hulton Getty)

Following the passage of the Kansas–Nebraska Act in 1854, Free Soilers and supporters of slavery contended for control of the territory. Several years of violence claimed hundreds of casualties and presaged the much larger sectional strife that soon engulfed the nation. In this photograph, Free Soilers stand beside a small cannon. Kansas entered the Union as a free state in 1861. (Kansas State Historical Society, Topeka, Kansas)

considered northerners a cold, grasping people who cared little about family and subordinated everything to the pursuit of money and material goods. They also believed northerners too quick to judge others, insistent on forcing their reforming beliefs on all Americans, and intent on meddling with a southern society dependent on slavery to exert social and economic control over black people.

Sectional crisis looms

The sectional crisis assumed its most aggravated form in connection with territorial expansion. Aware of its growing inferiority in population, the South believed it necessary to match the North state for state. This would maintain parity in the United States Senate, where each state had two representatives regardless of population. The North, equally cognisant of its edge in population, insisted that it should wield greater influence in government. White southerners also asserted that their "peculiar institution," as slavery was called, must be able to expand into the new areas lest their economy stagnate. Beginning in the late 1840s, large numbers of northerners supported a free soil movement that sought to prevent slavery's introduction into federal territories. Many of those calling for free soil in the West, it should be noted, were as racist as any southern slaveholder. They envisioned territories reserved for free white men and their families.

    A number of mileposts marked the road of sectional friction. In 1820, the Missouri Compromise restricted slavery in the Louisiana Purchase country to land below latitude 36° 30" N . Missouri entered the Union as a slave state and Maine as a free

improving society. Reform movements found little fertile ground in the South, and by the 1850s most white southerners had adopted a stance affirming slavery as a "positive good" for both masters and those held in bondage.

    Slavery served not only as a form of labor control, but also as the key to the South's social order. Only about one-third of white southern families owned slaves, and most of those held fewer than five. Just 12 percent of the slaveholders owned 12 or more slaves, the dividing line often given between a plantation and a farm. But all white southerners had a stake in the system of slavery because, as white people, they belonged to the region's controlling class. No matter how wretched their condition, they were superior, in their minds and according to the social and legal structure of southern society, to the millions of enslaved black people. White southerners, regardless of economic status, were made equal by the fact of black slavery. For this reason, and because of genuine fear of what would happen should large numbers of free black people be loosed upon the South, white southerners saw slavery as a necessary and generally beneficent institution, and reacted very defensively to criticism from the North.

    By the late antebellum years, many white southerners had developed a strong set of stereotypes about the North. They

state, thereby preserving the balance of power in the Senate and setting a precedent for admitting free and slave states in pairs that would hold for the next 30 years. Alarmed by hot congressional debates over Missouri, the aged Thomas Jefferson likened the issue to a "firebell in the night" and "considered it at once as the knell of the Union." In 1831, Nat Turner's bloody slave uprising in Southside Virginia and the founding of William Lloyd Garrison's abolitionist newspaper *The Liberator* spawned concern among white southerners. The admission of Texas as a slave state in 1845 and the war with Mexico in 1846–48 brought vast new western lands into the Union. The North staked out its position in 1846 with the Wilmot Proviso, which called for excluding slavery from all territory taken from Mexico. The Proviso, which passed the House of Representatives but failed in the Senate, served warning to the South that a good part of the North meant to bar slavery from all new territories.

Crisis followed crisis rapidly after 1848, a year in which the Free Soil Party mounted a major ticket for the presidency. The Compromise of 1850 admitted California as a free state, ending the South's parity in the Senate, and forced a tough fugitive slave law on the North. Two years later, publication of Harriet Beecher Stowe's anti-slavery novel *Uncle Tom's Cabin* reached a huge audience in the North and in England, winning untold converts to the abolitionist cause. The Kansas–Nebraska Act of 1854 sought to apply the doctrine of "popular sovereignty," which allowed the people of a territory, rather than the federal government, to decide whether they would accept slavery. Northerners argued that this violated the Missouri Compromise by reopening to slavery parts of the Louisiana Purchase territory. Virtual civil war erupted in Kansas, as slaveholders and free-staters fought to gain control of the area. More ominously for the North, the Supreme Court's Dred Scott decision in 1857 seemingly guaranteed a slaveholder's right to take chattels anywhere in the territories and possibly anywhere in

the free states. Outraged northerners denounced the Dred Scott outcome as proof that a "slave power conspiracy" in government gave the South clout far out of proportion to its population.

In the 1840s and 1850s, crucial national institutions failed to cope with increasing sectional tensions. Several Protestant denominations, including the Baptists and Methodists, split into northern and southern wings over the issue of slavery. The Whig Party broke apart in the early 1850s, its southern and northern wings hopelessly at odds. Meanwhile, the Democratic Party became in effect a southern-dominated sectional party. The Republican Party first ran a presidential candidate in 1856, its platform calling for a total ban on slavery in the territories. White southerners quickly associated Republicans with abolitionists—though the two were by no means synonymous. In the minds of many in the North, the Democratic Party served as a mere tool of the slaveocracy, its northern members, such as presidents Franklin Pierce and James Buchanan, derisively called "doughfaces" who did the bidding of their southern masters.

Perceptions on each side had reached a point by the mid-1850s that scarcely allowed many northerners or southerners to view the other section sympathetically or even realistically. Each side expected the worst from the other. The white South looked north and saw a nation of abolitionists intent on killing the institution that lay at the foundation of southern economics and society. The North looked south and saw a land of aggressive slaveholders who used the national courts and doughface allies in the presidency and Congress to frustrate the nation's progress towards greatness as a free labor, capitalist state. By 1859, a great many people in the North and the South had formed opinions that would make compromise difficult if another major crisis should arise. When the presidential election of 1860 propelled into power a party that had called for closing the territories to slavery, just such a crisis had arrived.

Election; Southern secession; creation of the Confederacy

The opening scene of the crisis of 1860–61 took place in the autumn of 1859. On October 16, John Brown and a small band of followers seized the federal arsenal at Harpers Ferry, Virginia, as part of a plan to gather slaves in a mountain stronghold, arm them and wage war on the South's slaveholders. Robert E. Lee and a detachment of United States Marines quickly suppressed the raiders, and Brown himself was tried, sentenced to die, and hanged. Comporting himself with dignity and courage at his trial and execution, Brown won the admiration of much of the North. As he went to the gallows, he handed one of his jailers a note that read, "I John Brown am now quite *certain* that the crimes of this *guilty, land*: *will* never be purged *away*; but with Blood." In the North, a number of newspapers praised Brown, church bells peeled his honor and other such demonstrations underscored that a substantial element of the northern public shared, at least to a degree, Brown's hatred of slavery.

White southerners, in contrast, reacted in horror at both Brown's actions and the northern response. Here was a man who had planned to incite a full-scale slave rebellion that would trigger a bloodbath and leave the South in chaos. Assurances from northern Democrats that they repudiated Brown's raid fell on deaf ears. White southerners equated Brown with abolitionists, abolitionists with Republicans, and Republicans with the whole North. A wave of near hysteria swept the South, the greatest since Nat Turner's rebellion some 30 years earlier. Slave patrols were increased, volunteer military companies drilled more seriously, and talk of secession mushroomed. William L. Yancey of Alabama, one of the extreme advocates of southern rights known as "fire-eaters," used heightened fears of northern aggression to persuade his state's Democratic Party to instruct delegates

With his flowing beard and thick shock of hair, John Brown reminded many northern admirers of an Old Testament prophet. White southerners took a very different view of Brown, who stood among the most implacable and violent foes of slavery. Frederick Douglass, the famous black abolitionist, commented that Brown's "will impressed all." (Author's collection)

to the 1860 national convention to demand a plank calling for protection of slavery in all national territories. Other states of the Lower South (Florida, Georgia, Louisiana, Mississippi, South Carolina and Texas) might be expected to follow Alabama's lead.

Election of Abraham Lincoln

The Democratic convention met in Charleston, South Carolina, in April 1860. A hotbed of secessionist sentiment, Charleston witnessed a contentious series of debates. Northern Democrats rejected a proposed platform that embodied Yancey's demands, several dozen southern delegates walked out and the convention adjourned without a nomination. The Democrats reconvened in Baltimore in mid-June, but failed again to agree on a platform. The regular Democrats, who comprised the majority of the party, ultimately nominated Senator Stephen A. Douglas of Illinois, a supporter of popular sovereignty, while southern rights Democrats selected slaveholder John C. Breckinridge of Kentucky to bear their standard. As the election approached, the Democratic Party, long the dominant force in American national politics, lay in a shambles.

The Republicans had met in Chicago in mid-May and chosen Abraham Lincoln as their presidential candidate. A moderate, Lincoln fully supported a platform that would prohibit slavery in the territories but accept the institution in states where it already existed. The platform further called for measures that expressed the mercantile, pro-business, free labor sentiments of many in the North.

A fourth candidate, nominated by voters calling themselves the Constitutional Union Party, also entered the field. He was John Bell, an old Whig from the state of Tennessee. Hoping to avoid the poisonous influence of issues related to slavery, the Constitutional Union Party based its campaign strictly on support of the Constitution, the laws of the United States and the sacred Union.

The election broke down into a contest between Lincoln and Douglas in the North and Breckinridge and Bell in the South. The Republicans did not appear on the ballot in ten slave states, and Bell and Breckinridge stood no chance of winning any of the free states. During the course of the campaign, many leaders from the Lower South threatened secession in the event of a Republican victory. Republicans responded that the South had postured about secession in the past, and they vowed not to give in to any southern demands. Outpolled by nearly a million popular votes, Lincoln and the Republicans achieved a decisive victory in the Electoral College, taking 180 votes to the other three candidates' 123. Lincoln did especially well in the upper sections of the North, where anti-slavery sentiment was strongest, polling about 60 percent of the votes. He managed a bare majority elsewhere in the North. Breckinridge carried the Lower South and four states of the Upper South. Bell won in Virginia, Kentucky and Tennessee. Douglas showed poorly, winning just 12 electoral votes in New Jersey and Missouri—which showed how sectionalism had ravaged the proud old Democratic Party.

Secession begins

Contrary to those who believed they were bluffing, secessionists in the Lower South moved quickly after Lincoln's election. South Carolina led the way, calling a convention that voted unanimously on December 20, 1860 to leave the Union. Over the next six weeks, following debates of varying intensity between those for and against secession, Mississippi (January 9, 1861), Florida (January 10), Alabama (January 11), Georgia (January 19), Louisiana (January 26), and Texas (February 1) also seceded. The seven states created the Confederate States of America at a convention in Montgomery, Alabama, in February and March 1861. Adopting a constitution much like that of the United States but with explicit guarantees for slavery and stronger

Jefferson Davis believed ardently in slavery and southern rights, but he was not a "fire-eater." These qualities, together with his stature as a prominent United States senator, made him an attractive figure to the delegates in Montgomery, Alabama. Although frequently compared unfavorably to Abraham Lincoln, Davis proved to be an able chief executive for the new slaveholding republic. He lacked Lincoln's genius with language, but dealt forcefully with the staggering challenge of simultaneously launching a nation and waging a war. (Author's collection)

overwhelming magnitude imperiled," added Davis, "the people of the Southern States were driven by the conduct of the North to the adoption of some course of action to avert the danger with which they were openly menaced."

The secession of the Lower South represented a gambling effort to protect the institution of slavery in the face of a striking defeat at the polls. Many slaveholders looked down the road and saw ever larger numbers of free states controlling both houses of Congress, Republican justices on the Supreme Court and a national government willing to tolerate or even encourage agitators such as John Brown.

provisions for state powers, the founders of the new nation selected Jefferson Davis of Mississippi and Alexander H. Stephens of Georgia as President and Vice-President respectively.

Davis and Stephens emphasized the centrality of slavery to the process of secession. In a speech delivered on March 21, 1861, Stephens averred that the Confederate constitution "has put at rest *forever* all the agitating question relating to our peculiar institutions—African slavery as it exists among us—the proper *status* of the negro in our form of civilization. *This was the immediate cause of the late rupture and present revolution.*" Five weeks later, Davis observed in a message to the Confederate Congress that slave labor "was and is indispensable" to southern economic progress. "With interests of such

South Carolina had threatened secession more than once prior to the crisis of 1860, most recently in response to the Compromise of 1850. Many northerners believed that secessionist talk in South Carolina after Lincoln's election amounted to mere posturing. This broadside sent a clear message that those who sought to take the state out of the Union had triumphed. (Library of Congress)

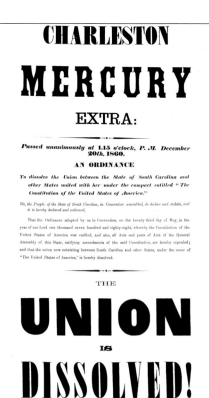

CHARLESTON
MERCURY
EXTRA:

Passed unanimously at 1.15 o'clock, P. M. December 20th, 1860.

AN ORDINANCE

To dissolve the Union between the State of South Carolina and other States united with her under the compact entitled "The Constitution of the United States of America."

We, the People of the State of South Carolina, in Convention assembled, do declare and ordain, and it is hereby declared and ordained,

That the Ordinance adopted by us in Convention, on the twenty third day of May, in the year of our Lord one thousand seven hundred and eighty-eight, whereby the Constitution of the United States of America was ratified, and also, all Acts and parts of Acts of the General Assembly of this State, ratifying amendments of the said Constitution, are hereby repealed; and that the union now subsisting between South Carolina and other States, under the name of "The United States of America," is hereby dissolved.

THE
UNION
IS
DISSOLVED!

The United States in 1860

Of the 15 slave states, Missouri, Kentucky, Maryland and Delaware remained loyal to the Union. Numbers in the 11 Confederate states indicate the order in which they seceded.

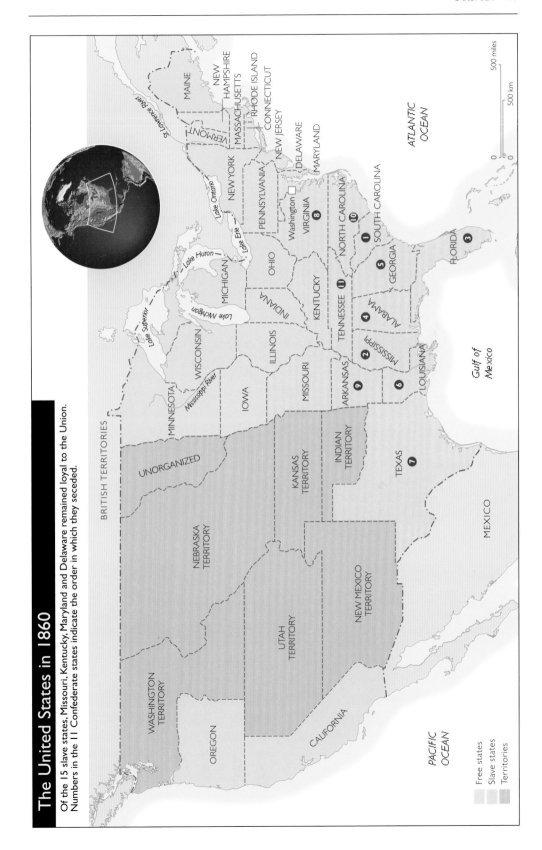

Free states
Slave states
Territories

Fort Sumter

Democratic President James Buchanan remained in office nearly two and a half months after the secession of South Carolina. Eight slave states remained in the Union, all of them disinclined to join their Lower South brethren. Buchanan refused to accept the legitimacy of secession, but also said he would do nothing to force the wayward states back into the Union. He watched helplessly as the Confederate states seized federal installations and property, prompting a furious barrage of criticism from Republicans. Many of Buchanan's critics overlooked the fact that Unionists in the Upper South typically made it clear that they would remain loyal only as long as the incoming Lincoln administration guaranteed the safety of slavery in states where it already

existed and, more ominously, employed no coercion against the seceded states.

The question of coercion came to focus on Fort Sumter, a federal stronghold in Charleston harbor. In his inaugural address of March 4, 1861, Lincoln sought to place responsibility for the start of hostilities on Jefferson Davis and the Confederates. Lincoln announced his intention to "hold, occupy, and possess the property, and places belonging to the government, and to collect the duties and imposts; but beyond what may be necessary for these objects, there will

Confederates occupied Fort Sumter immediately after Robert Anderson's small garrison surrendered. In this engraving based on a photograph, the "stars and bars" float atop a makeshift flagpole attached to a derrick used for hoisting cannons to the fort's upper tier. Fort Sumter remained a defiant symbol of Confederate nationhood until the very last days of the conflict. (Author's collection)

be no invasion—no using of force against, or among the people anywhere." Turning directly to the question of responsibility for any aggressive moves, Lincoln added: "In *your* hands, my dissatisfied fellow countrymen, and not in *mine*, is the momentous issue of civil war. The government will not assail *you*. You can have no conflict, without yourselves being the aggressors." This statement left deliberately murky what Lincoln meant by "occupy and possess"—most federal holdings in the Confederate states had long since been lost. Lincoln mainly sought to gain time in the hope that Unionist sentiment would assert itself across the South and reverse the secessionist tide.

But time ran out. President Buchanan had previously refused to abandon Fort Sumter and sent a ship with reinforcements for the small garrison commanded by Major Robert Anderson. Southern batteries had fired on that vessel on January 9, 1861, prompting both sides to bluster and posture before drawing up short of open hostilities. Since that incident, Sumter had become a tremendously important symbol. Northerners saw it as the last significant installation in the Confederacy still in national hands, and Republicans adamantly refused to give it up. Confederates just as adamantly insisted that it stood on South Carolina soil and must be transferred to their control.

Major Anderson informed Lincoln in early March that the garrison's supplies would soon be exhausted. Convinced that the North would not tolerate loss of the fort, the President decided to send an unarmed ship with provisions. A full-scale effort to supply and reinforce the fort, Lincoln believed, would cast the North as the aggressor and almost certainly send the Upper South out of the Union. If Confederates fired on the unarmed ship, the North would appear as the injured party. Lincoln informed the governor of South Carolina that provisions were on the way and that the United States would not fire unless fired upon by southern batteries around Charleston harbor.

Jefferson Davis and the Confederate cabinet faced a serious dilemma. They also hoped to avoid the label of aggressor. Yet public opinion in the Confederacy overwhelmingly favored seizing Fort Sumter. Davis decided to request surrender of the fort before the relief vessel arrived. Anderson refused to capitulate, however, and shortly after 4.30 AM on April 12 southern guns opened fire. Anderson and his men surrendered 36 hours later. They left the fort with colors flying and to the accompaniment of a 50-gun salute, climbed aboard ships and sailed for the North. The next day, Lincoln issued a proclamation that declared a state of insurrection and called out 75,000 militia from the northern states.

War fever

War fever swept across the North and South. In four states of the Upper South, all of which had previously decided against secession, Lincoln's call for militia galvanized sentiment. Virginia left the Union on April 17, Arkansas on May 6, North Carolina on May 20, and Tennessee on June 8. The Confederacy soon moved its capital from Montgomery to Richmond, Virginia, and the loss to the Union of these four states virtually assured a long and difficult war. Virginia, Tennessee and North Carolina ranked first, second and third in white population among the Confederate states. They also possessed more than half of the new nation's manufacturing capacity, produced half its crops, contained nearly half its horses and mules and, most tellingly, would provide nearly 40 percent of the Confederacy's soldiers.

Eleven of the 15 slave states had reacted decisively to the seismic events that had rocked the nation between the election of 1860 and Lincoln's call for volunteers. In withdrawing from the Union, white southerners set the stage for a war that would test the strength of the American republic and destroy forever the social structure they had hoped to preserve.

Strengths and weaknesses of the Union and the Confederacy

The North entered the war with seemingly decisive advantages in almost every measurable category. This has led to a common perception, often rooted in analysis that begins with the Confederate surrender at Appomattox and works backwards, that the South faced such overwhelming odds as to make victory impossible. A corollary to this idea suggests that the Confederacy managed to fight as long as it did only because of superior generalship and a gallant effort on the part of its common folk inside and outside the army. In fact, either side could have won the war, as an assessment of the contestants' strengths and weaknesses suggests.

Strengths of the North

The North did enjoy a number of advantages. The 1860 census placed the population of the United States at about 31,500,000. Of these, the 11 Confederate states had about 9,100,000—5,450,000 of whom were white, 3,500,000 slaves and 130,000 free black people. The North boasted a population of about 22,400,000. A number of factors somewhat altered these basic figures. A number of white people in states remaining loyal to the Union—especially the slaveholding Border States of Missouri, Kentucky, Maryland and Delaware—supported the Confederacy. Conversely, many white residents of the Confederacy—especially in the mountain areas of western Virginia, western North Carolina, eastern Tennessee and parts of Alabama, Texas and Arkansas—remained loyal to the Union. Moreover, about 150,000 black men from the Confederate states eventually served in the Union army. That slaves did not carry arms for the Confederacy was offset by the fact

that their labor freed a disproportionate number of white southern males to fight. With all factors taken into consideration, the North enjoyed about a 5–2 edge in manpower. Roughly 2,100,000 men fought for the Union (roughly 50 percent of the military-age male population), while between 800,000 and 900,000 served in the Confederate army (nearly 80 percent of the 1860 military-age males).

Hundreds of thousands of men volunteered on each side during the first few months of the war, after which enlistment fell off sharply. Both sides eventually resorted to national conscription (the Confederates a year earlier than the United States), though some men continued to enlist freely until the end of the conflict. Little separated the two sides in terms of the quality and potential of their volunteers. Haphazard training left many thousands of men woefully unprepared for the rigors of active campaigning. Units led by West Point graduates or other officers with military experience fared better than those commanded by volunteers whose enthusiasm far exceeded their expertise. Volunteer officers and enlisted men learned their craft together in camp, on the march and in the unforgiving crucible of combat.

The North far outstripped the Confederacy in almost every economic category. A few comparative figures suggest the degree of northern superiority. In 1860, there were 110,000 northern manufacturing establishments employing 1,300,000 workers; in the Confederate states, just 18,000 establishments employing 110,000 workers. Northern railroad mileage totalled nearly 22,000 compared with just over 9,000 in the Confederacy, and the northern roads generally were more modern and better maintained. The North produced

These members of the Sumter Light Guards of Americus, Georgia, were typical of the hundreds of thousands of men who joined infantry companies following the outbreak of war. The photographer posed them in Augusta, Georgia, in April 1861, while they were *en route* to join the Confederate army in Virginia. The Guards became Company K of the 4th Georgia Infantry and saw extensive action. (Library of Congress)

97 per cent of the nation's firearms in 1860, held more than 80 per cent of the national bank deposits, accounted for more than 85 per cent of capital invested in industry and manufactured 15 times as much iron as the Confederate states and virtually all of the nation's textiles (though heavily dependent on southern cotton) and shoes and boots. There were 800,000 draft animals in the North compared with just 300,000 in the Confederate states—a tremendous logistical advantage in an era when armies moved by horse and mule power. In agricultural production, the two sides stood roughly at parity in terms of the ratio of production to overall population.

A third northern advantage lay in the area of professional military forces. Lincoln's government began the conflict with an army and a navy, while the Davis administration had to build from scratch. But the United States army numbered only about 14,000 in the spring of 1861 (many southern officers had resigned to support the Confederacy) and lay scattered across the country in small posts, many of them in the vast trans-Mississippi territories. Like the Confederacy, the North had to build huge armies of volunteers with no previous military experience. The North initially kept the regular units together rather than parcelling out veterans among volunteer units, thus limiting the nation's soldiering expertise to a handful of regiments.

The United States navy began the conflict with only 42 ships in commission, most of which patrolled waters far from the American coast. In the spring of 1861, when Lincoln declared a blockade of the Confederacy, only three vessels were available for immediate service along the southern coast. Moreover, the United States navy was a deep-water force with little expertise in the type of coastal and offshore operations that would be required to suppress the southern rebellion. Still, the navy must be reckoned a northern advantage because the Confederacy possessed no naval force at the opening of the conflict and lacked the industrial base to construct modern warships.

Strengths of the South

The Confederacy also entered the war with decided advantages. Perhaps the greatest lay in requisite conditions for victory. The Confederacy had only to defend itself to achieve independence, whereas the North faced the prospect of invading the South, destroying its capacity to wage war and crushing the Confederate people's will to resist. The Confederacy could win by default if the northern people chose not to expend the human and material resources necessary to fight a modern war. If the North did commit to a major conflict, the Confederacy could triumph by prolonging the contest to a point where the northern populace considered the effort too costly in lives and national treasure. The American Revolution offered an obvious example of how the colonies (with vital assistance from France) had faced daunting material disadvantages against Great Britain, but had won by dragging the war out and exhausting the British commitment to win.

Defending home soil conveyed other advantages to the Confederates. Soldiers protecting hearth and family typically exhibit higher morale than invaders, and Confederates often had a better grasp of topography and local roads. Friendly civilians provided information to southern officers, as when a local man helped Thomas J. "Stonewall" Jackson find a route that would allow his command to launch its famous flank attack at the Battle of Chancellorsville on May 2, 1863.

Geography promised an overall military advantage to the South. The Confederacy spread over more than 750,000 square miles (1,942,500 square kilometers), much of it beyond the reach of good roads or rail lines. A 3,500-mile (5,630 km) coastline contained nearly 200 harbors and navigable river mouths, and Texas shared an open border with Mexico—features that rendered a truly crippling Union blockade nearly impossible.

General Pierre Gustave Toutant Beauregard commanded the bombardment of Fort Sumter and became an early Confederate military idol. A native of Louisiana whose first language was French, he graduated second in the West Point class of 1838 and served with distinction in the war with Mexico. Somewhat given to grandiose strategic planning, he held a succession of important commands in various theaters during the Civil War. (Author's collection)

In Virginia, the Shenandoah valley offered a protected corridor through which Confederate armies could march to threaten Washington and other parts of the North, and several rivers that flowed generally west to east presented potential barriers to Union overland movements against the southern capital. On the negative side for the Confederacy, the North could use these same rivers as waterborne avenues of advance.

Aware that material factors favored their opponents, many Confederates nevertheless understood their own strong points and appreciated the magnitude of the North's challenge. For example, George Wythe Randolph, a Virginian who served as a brigadier-general and Secretary of War, commented in the autumn of 1861 that Union forces "may overrun our frontier States and plunder our coast but, as for conquering us, the thing is an impossibility." Randolph believed that history offered no instance of "a people as numerous as we are inhabiting a country so extensive as ours being subjected if true to themselves." General P. G. T. Beauregard similarly remarked after the war that no "people ever warred for independence with more relative advantages than the Confederates," among which he noted geography well suited to blocking Union invasions. "If, as a military question, they [the Confederate people] must have failed," concluded Beauregard, "then no country must aim at freedom by means of war."

A persistent myth about the Civil War holds that the Confederacy enjoyed better generalship. Such a view makes sense if applied only to the Eastern Theater in the first two years of the war. The Army of Northern Virginia, under the guidance of Robert E. Lee and a talented cast of subordinates who included Stonewall Jackson and James Longstreet, won a series of dramatic victories in 1862–63 that created an aura of magnificent accomplishment. Overall, however, North and South drew on very similar pools of officers. West Pointers held most of the top positions in all Civil War armies, and they shared a common heritage. They took the same courses from the same professors at the academy, learned the same lessons in class and on battlefields in Mexico, and tended to subscribe to the same strategic and tactical theories. They understood the dominance of the tactical defensive because of the increased killing range of rifle muskets and the value of field fortifications. They therefore tried to avoid direct assaults by turning an enemy's flank (which often proved impossible). They also sought to operate on interior lines both strategically and tactically. Some generals proved more adept at translating these ideas into action, but most Civil War campaigns and battles were based on them. Apart from the West Pointers, both sides appointed some political generals and saw a few untutored officers achieve substantial fame.

The Confederacy seemed to have a clear advantage in their Commander-in-Chief. Jefferson Davis was a West Point graduate who had commanded a regiment in the war with Mexico and later served as Secretary of War. Abraham Lincoln's military credentials consisted of a short stint as a volunteer junior officer during the Black Hawk war of the 1830s. But Lincoln learned quickly, and he and Davis both exhibited a sound grasp of strategy as well as military theory and practice.

One variable could throw off the entire equation. The possibility of foreign intervention, particularly by Great Britain or France, received enormous attention from both governments and the northern and Confederate people. The example of the American Revolution once again stood out. Intervention along the lines of French participation in the Revolutionary War could yield profound military and economic consequences.

In summary, the North entered the war with a range of considerable advantages, but the Confederacy by no means faced a hopeless struggle. Other nations had won against longer odds. In the end, it would come down to which side mustered its human and material resources more effectively, found the better military and political leaders, and managed to sustain popular support for the war effort.

From First Manassas to Chancellorsville

After the secession of Virginia and the transfer of the Confederate capital to Richmond, both sides sought to mobilize men and resources and devise their military strategies. The North faced the prospect of mounting an active campaign to compel the Confederate states to return to the Union, while the Confederacy had the easier task of responding to northern movements. If Lincoln and his government proved unable to launch a major offensive, the Confederacy would win its independence by default.

Volunteers poured into both armies. The Confederate Congress passed laws in March and May 1861 authorizing the enrollment of 500,000 men (from a pool of roughly 1,000,000 military-age white males), and hundreds of thousands stepped forward. About half volunteered for three years and the rest for 12 months. The North drew roughly 700,000 men into its forces during the initial rush to the colors, most of them for three years' service.

The basic unit of organization on both sides was the company, which on paper contained 100 men. Ten companies made up a regiment, four or more regiments a brigade, two or more brigades a division, and two or more divisions a corps (the Confederacy did not officially have corps until the autumn of 1862). Companies tended to be raised from a single locality, and many regiments came from one town or county. Locally prominent individuals served as company and regimental officers. In terms of drill and discipline, regiments with a West Pointer, a graduate of military colleges such as the Virginia Military Institute, or a veteran of the war with Mexico typically progressed far more rapidly than those dependent entirely on civilian officers.

Strategic planning proceeded apace with volunteering. General-in-Chief Winfield Scott coordinated Union planning. Born in 1786, hero of the second war against Great Britain in 1812 and the war with Mexico in the 1840s, and the Whig Party's nominee for President in 1852, Scott was in the final stage of an illustrious career. He had cut an imposing figure as a younger man, a full 6 feet 5 inches tall, immaculately dressed and of flawless military bearing. Ulysses S. Grant described him in the 1840s as "the finest specimen of manhood my eyes had ever beheld, and the most to be envied." By 1861, Scott suffered from an array of ailments and weighed more than 300lb (135kg), but his mind remained strong and in April and May he formulated a long-range plan for defeating the Confederacy.

Known as the "Anaconda Plan" because it aimed to squeeze the Confederacy to death, Scott's strategic blueprint called for a vigorous movement down the Mississippi river by a naval flotilla and an army of 80,000. Union control of the Mississippi would split the Confederacy into two pieces, while other naval forces would blockade southern ports and cut off supplies from the outside world. Should the Confederacy continue to resist after losing the Mississippi and its key ports, Scott believed a major invasion would be necessary. Such an operation would consume two or three years and require a force of up to 300,000 soldiers. Scott took a realistic view of campaigning with volunteer soldiers. The initial strike down the Mississippi could not begin earlier than the autumn of 1861, he insisted, due to the need to muster the recruits, train them for several months and prepare the logistical effort.

The old General's planning, which in many respects anticipated the way the war would be conducted, soon ran foul of politics and public opinion. Scott worried

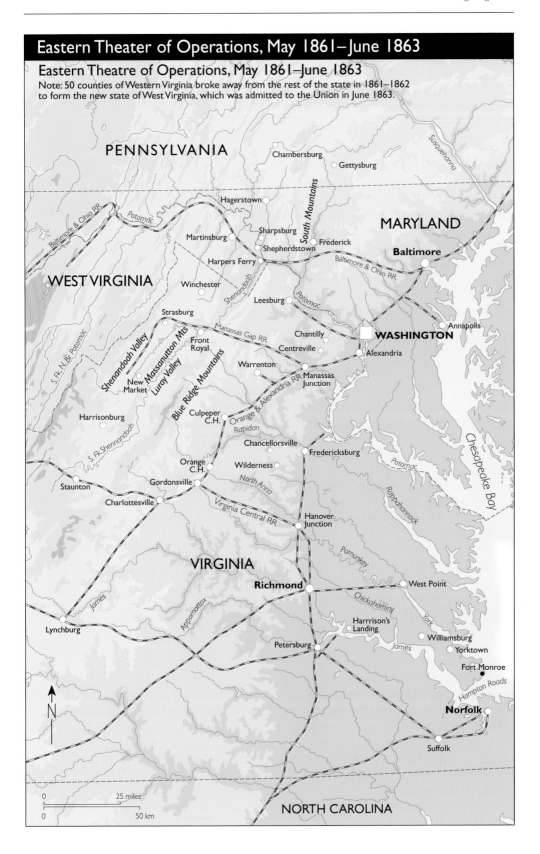

Eastern Theater of Operations, May 1861– June 1863

Eastern Theatre of Operations, May 1861–June 1863

Note: 50 counties of Western Virginia broke away from the rest of the state in 1861–1862 to form the new state of West Virginia, which was admitted to the Union in June 1863.

that the northern people would demand an immediate invasion of the Confederacy to extinguish the rebellion, and his fears soon proved to be well grounded. When the Confederacy moved its capital to Richmond, just 100 miles (160 km) separated the two seats of government. Ignorant of the staggering task of equipping and training an army, northerners clamoured for an immediate campaign against Richmond. This began a pattern that held for the remainder of the war. Many in the North, both civilians and political leaders, exhibited a preoccupation with Richmond rooted in a belief that its capture would destroy the Confederacy. This preoccupation in turn helped make northern and central Virginia by far the bloodiest battleground of the war.

Battle of First Manassas or Bull Run

At a meeting on June 29, 1861, Abraham Lincoln listened to his military and political advisers discuss strategy. Brigadier-General Irvin McDowell, a 42-year-old West Pointer who had served his entire career in staff positions and enjoyed excellent political connections, commanded Union troops near Washington. He urged an attack against a Confederate force known to be in position 25 miles (40 km) south-west of Washington near Manassas Junction. Scott opposed McDowell, arguing for "a war of large bodies" rather than "a little war by piece-meal." Lincoln and the cabinet supported McDowell, approving an advance to begin on July 9. Meanwhile, northern newspapers called for a quick movement into Virginia. The *New York Tribune* trumpeted: "Forward to Richmond! Forward to Richmond!—The Rebel Congress must not be allowed to meet there on the 20th of July! By that date the place must be held by the National Army!" On July 16, a week past the date originally set, McDowell put his army in motion towards Manassas Junction.

Four armies played roles in the campaign. Near Winchester in the lower Shenandoah valley (rivers flow south-west to north-east in the valley, so the northern section is called the lower valley), Joseph E. Johnston commanded about 12,000 soldiers who guarded the north-west flank of Confederate forces in Virginia. Opposite Johnston, near Harpers Ferry, Robert Patterson led nearly 18,000 Union troops. A veteran of the war of 1812, the aged Patterson had orders to watch Johnston and prevent his movement out of the valley to link up with P. G. T. Beauregard's 20,000 Confederates near Manassas Junction. McDowell's 35,000 men, the largest American field army to that point in history, marched to strike Beauregard before Johnston could reinforce him. The Confederate forces enjoyed the strategic advantage of the Manassas Gap Railroad, which ran from Beauregard's position to a point slightly south of Johnston's.

McDowell's green troops moved slowly towards Manassas, exhibiting lax discipline while consuming two and a half days in a 20-mile (32 km) march to Centreville.

A native of Virginia who remained loyal to the Union, Winfield Scott ranks among the most accomplished soldiers in United States history. Scott's brilliant march from Vera Cruz to Mexico City in 1847 impressed the Duke of Wellington. "His campaign was unsurpassed in military annals," observed the Duke. "He is the greatest living soldier." (Author's collection)

Confederate civilians alerted Beauregard
about the Union advance, and on July 17 he
sent a message asking Johnston to join him
and help "crush the enemy." Johnston had
become convinced that the timid Patterson,
who imagined himself badly outnumbered
and refused to take decisive action, posed no
serious threat. When orders arrived from
Richmond early on July 18 urging him to
support Beauregard if practicable, Johnston
began shifting his troops towards a loading
point on the Manassas Gap Railroad. The
bulk of Johnston's force made the trip to
Manassas over the next 48 hours, completing
the first large-scale movement of troops by
rail in an active campaign.

After inconclusive skirmishing on July 18,
Beauregard and McDowell each developed
plans to hit the other's left flank on the 21st.
Beauregard had placed the Confederates
along the western bank of Bull Run, a
sluggish stream to the north and west of
Manassas Junction. Although outranked by
Johnston, Beauregard maintained tactical
control and planned to hold his left with a
light force while massing his strength against
McDowell's left. McDowell planned a
demonstration against the southern right as
a strong flanking force crossed Bull Run in
the vicinity of Sudley Ford and sought to roll
up the enemy's line along the creek.

The Union soldiers, or Federals, struck
first on July 21. After a fumbling advance
towards Sudley Springs, northern troops
under General David Hunter collided with
Colonel Nathan G. Evans's brigade of
South Carolina and Louisiana troops.
Reinforcements came forward to support
both sides, and a bitter struggle for control
of Matthews Hill, a prominent knob on the
Manassas–Sudley road, raged between about
10 and 11:30 AM. The arrival of Union
brigades under Colonels William Tecumseh
Sherman and Erasmus Keyes eventually
compelled the Confederates to abandon
Matthews Hill and take up a position south
of the Warrenton Turnpike on Henry Hill.

Beauregard and Johnston had abandoned
all thoughts of a blow against McDowell's
left. As Federals gathered themselves along

Irvin McDowell impressed many of his contemporaries
more as a gourmand than as a military leader. Often
tentative in the field, he acted more decisively at the
table. A staff officer who dined with the General in 1861
described him as "so absorbed in the dishes before him
that he had but little time for conversation … he
gobbled the larger portion of every dish within reach,
and wound up with an entire watermelon, which he
said was 'monstrous fine!'" (Author's collection)

A West Point classmate of Robert E. Lee, Joseph
E. Johnston compiled a dazzling record during the war
with Mexico and left the United States army in 1861 as
a brigadier-general of staff. Always envious of his fellow
Virginian Lee, Johnston garnered neither the public
adulation nor the professional acclaim he believed his
Confederate service deserved. (Author's collection)

the Warrenton Turnpike for a final push against Henry Hill, Confederates sought to knit together a stable defensive line. Among the southern troops going into position was a brigade of five Virginia regiments led by Brigadier-General Thomas Jonathan Jackson. This dour Virginian, a graduate of West Point in 1846, had fought with distinction in Mexico and later taught at the Virginia Military Institute. As Jackson's soldiers went into position on Henry Hill, Brigadier-General Barnard Bee of South Carolina, whose brigade had fought on Matthew's Hill, remarked that the enemy "are beating us back." "Sir," replied Jackson, "we will give them the bayonet."

Fighting swayed back and forth across the crest and along the slopes of Henry Hill between about 1:30 and 3:30 PM. Near the eye of the storm stood the home of Judith Carter Henry, an 85-year-old bedridden widow who became the only civilian killed during the battle (various accounts place the number of wounds she suffered as high as 13). Jackson's brigade played a major part in the action. At one point, General Bee approached a group of soldiers standing some distance behind Jackson's position and asked, "What regiment is this?" "Why General, don't you know your own men?" replied an officer. "This is what is left of the 4th Alabama." The men said they would follow Bee back into the fight, whereupon he pointed towards his left and shouted: "Yonder stands Jackson like a stone wall; let's go to his assistance." Thus was born the most famous soubriquet of the Civil War.

The climax on Henry Hill came at about 4 PM. Confederate brigades under Colonels Jubal A. Early, Arnold Elzey and Joseph B. Kershaw had hurried forward from Manassas Junction. The weight of their bayonets turned the tide, propelling exhausted Federals away from the high ground. "We scared the enemy worse than we hurt him," remarked Early later. "He had been repulsed, not routed. When, however, the retreat began, it soon degenerated into a rout from the panic-stricken fears of the enemy's troops." Beauregard next ordered a general advance. Hungry, thirsty, hot and without experience in such situations, thousands of Union troops decided they had seen enough. "The men seemed to be seized simultaneously by the conviction that it was no use to do anything more," observed a northern officer, "and they might as well start home."

The tide of humanity sweeping away from the battlefield included a number of people who had ridden out from Washington to watch the action. Soldiers discarded their weapons and pressed eastwards in the midst of cannons, caissons and wagons, jostling for position among civilians in fine carriages. Congressman Alfred Ely of New York was taken prisoner, barely escaping death at the hands of an infuriated South Carolina colonel who tried to shoot him. "He's a member of Congress, God damn him," raged the colonel. "Came out here to see the fun! Came to see us whipped and killed! God damn him! If it was not for such as he there would be no war. They've made it and then come to gloat over it! God damn him. I'll show him."

The Confederates made only a feeble effort to harry the retreating Federals. Although this failure would prompt a great deal of criticism, the southern army almost certainly lacked the discipline to mount an effective pursuit. Victory had left Johnston's and Beauregard's soldiers nearly as disorganized as their foe. By the end of the following day, McDowell's army had gathered itself near Washington. Any chance for a Confederate counterstroke had passed.

The Battle of First Manassas or Bull Run (Confederates called it the former, Federals the latter) set a new standard for bloodletting in American history. Union casualties totalled 2,896, and the Confederates lost 1,982 men. Carnage at later battles would dwarf these figures, but in July 1861 the respective nations viewed the battle as a ghastly affair. It foreshadowed later engagements in a number of respects. Both commanding generals sought to avoid frontal assaults by launching flank movements. The side with interior lines held an advantage, as the Confederates used the Manassas Gap Railroad to effect a

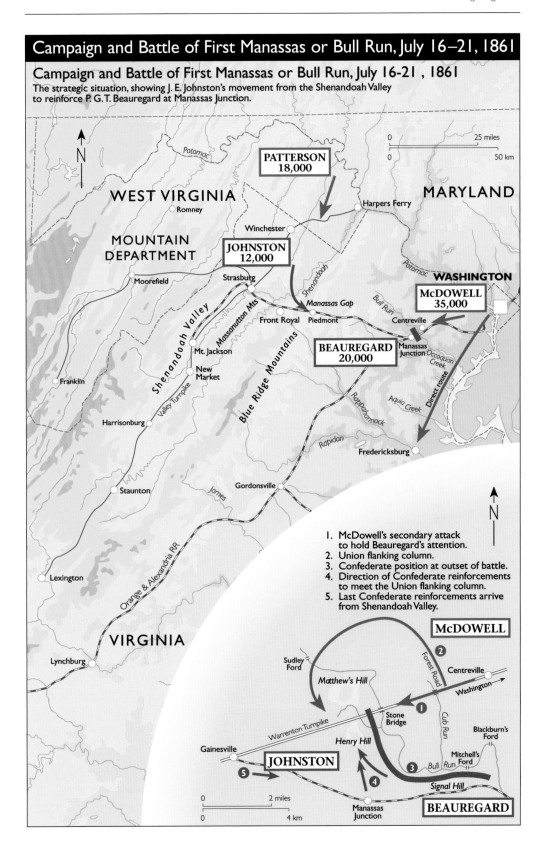

Campaign and Battle of First Manassas or Bull Run, July 16–21, 1861

Campaign and Battle of First Manassas or Bull Run, July 16-21 , 1861
The strategic situation, showing J. E. Johnston's movement from the Shenandoah Valley
to reinforce P. G. T. Beauregard at Manassas Junction.

WEST VIRGINIA

Romney

MOUNTAIN DEPARTMENT

Moorefield

Franklin

Harrisonburg

Staunton

Lexington

VIRGINIA

Lynchburg

PATTERSON 18,000

Harpers Ferry

MARYLAND

Winchester

JOHNSTON 12,000

Strasburg

Potomac

WASHINGTON

Manassas Gap

Front Royal   Piedmont

McDOWELL 35,000

Centreville

Mt. Jackson

New Market

BEAUREGARD 20,000

Manassas Junction

Occoquan Creek

Rappahannock

Aquia Creek

Direct route

Rapidan

Fredericksburg

Gordonsville

James

Orange & Alexandria RR

0   25 miles
0   50 km

1. McDowell's secondary attack to hold Beauregard's attention.
2. Union flanking column.
3. Confederate position at outset of battle.
4. Direction of Confederate reinforcements to meet the Union flanking column.
5. Last Confederate reinforcements arrive from Shenandoah Valley.

McDOWELL

Sudley Ford

Matthew's Hill

Forest Road

Centreville

Washington

Stone Bridge

Blackburn's Ford

Warrenton Turnpike

Henry Hill

Cub Run

Mitchell's Ford

Bull Run

Gainesville

JOHNSTON

Signal Hill

Manassas Junction

BEAUREGARD

0   2 miles
0   4 km

strategic concentration and later shifted troops from their right to their left along shorter tactical lines. Finally, the battle demonstrated the difficulty of achieving a truly decisive tactical triumph. Although battered and forced to retreat, the Union army remained intact.

The battle had a major impact on the home fronts. Northerners abandoned all hopes of a speedy end to the war. Subduing the rebels would be more difficult and costly than many had imagined. Confederates took heart, celebrating what they saw as the superiority of their fighting men. The battle remained prominent in the national consciousness for many months because no other major action occurred in Virginia until the spring of 1862.

Abraham Lincoln knew he had to replace McDowell after the ignominious result of

First Bull Run. He selected 34-year-old Major-General George Brinton McClellan to command the Union army near Washington. A West Pointer who finished second in the class of 1846, McClellan had earned distinction as an engineer during the war with Mexico, studied European military thinking and policies in the 1850s, and retired from the army to go into business in 1857. He returned to military service in April

British artist Frank Vizetelly witnessed the Union retreat at First Manassas, making this sketch for the *Illustrated London News.* "The terror-stricken soldiers threw away their arms and accoutrements," wrote Vizetelly disdainfully, "herding along like a panic-stricken flock of sheep, with no order whatever in their flight. Those who had been fortunate enough to get placed in the baggage-waggons thrust back others with their bayonets and musket-stocks."

1861 and won some modest victories in western Virginia early in the war. A man of medium height with large shoulders and a barrel chest, he dressed carefully and presented a thoroughly professional appearance. The northern press lauded him as a brilliant commander, which fed his considerable ego and led him to believe no one else could save the republic.

As a Democrat, McClellan opposed much of the Republican Party's legislative agenda and reserved some of his harshest criticism for Radical Republicans and abolitionists who sought to turn the war into a crusade against slavery. McClellan joined virtually all other northern Democrats (and most Republicans as well) in defining the conflict as a struggle to restore the Union rather than to free slaves. A member of his staff recalled McClellan's saying that anyone who expected him to wage war against the South "to *free the slaves* … would be mistaken, for he would not do it."

McClellan quickly revealed a deep contempt for most of his civilian and military superiors. He complained to his wife that General-in-Chief Scott got in his way. He called three members of the President's cabinet "an incompetent little puppy," a "garrulous old woman" and "an old fool." He dismissed Lincoln as "an idiot" and a "well-meaning baboon." On one occasion, he returned home to find that Lincoln and Secretary of State William Henry Seward had been waiting to see him. The General proceeded to go upstairs, sending word 30 minutes later that he had gone to bed and the two could come back another time.

Obnoxious personal qualities did not prevent McClellan from turning McDowell's demoralized soldiers into a formidable force. He christened them the Army of the

Potomac in August 1861, having expanded their number to more than 100,000, put them through a strict regimen of drill and instilled in them a strong sense of pride. Soldiers and officers alike responded with an outpouring of affection that made McClellan by far the most popular of all the generals who fought with the army.

Promotion came McClellan's way in early November 1861. A combination of infirmities and aggravation with McClellan prompted Winfield Scott to resign on November 1. "Little Mac," as the men called him, took Scott's place and added overall planning responsibility to his role as field commander of the Union's largest army. When Lincoln cautioned the General about juggling the many responsibilities of his two positions, McClellan answered, "I can do it all."

What he proved unwilling to do was move against Joseph E. Johnston's 45,000 Confederates in northern Virginia. McClellan grotesquely overestimated Johnston's strength, insisting that he needed 200,000 men to launch an offensive. To the end of his time in

Major-General George B. McClellan won the hearts of soldiers in the Army of the Potomac, but he lacked the stomach for the harsher aspects of war. "I am tired of the sickening sight of the battlefield," he wrote to Mrs. McClellan following his first real engagement at Seven Pines, "with its mangled corpses & poor suffering wounded! Victory has no charms for me when purchased at such cost." (Author's collection)

Thomas Jonathan Jackson in November 1862, in a photograph his wife considered an excellent likeness. During a two-month visit to the Confederacy in 1862, British traveller W. C. Corsan heard stories about the Presbyterian Jackson that reminded him of "Cromwell, or some old Covenanter. The same silent, brooding self reliance—the same iron will—the same tenacity of purpose ... all surrounded and tinged by the same almost fanatical mingling of incessant devotions with arduous duties." (Author's collection)

field command, McClellan inflated southern numbers and devised innumerable excuses for not advancing. In truth, he lacked the mental or moral courage to risk his great army in a major contest with the rebels. He always hedged his bets, refused to take chances, sought to have every detail perfect before engaging in battle, and thus cannot be counted among the war's leading generals.

Lincoln and McClellan engaged in a struggle of wills throughout the late summer and autumn of 1861. Under pressure from Republican politicians and newspaper editors to capture Richmond, the President pressed McClellan to no avail. Months slipped by with no action. McClellan surrounded himself with officers who shared his conservative political beliefs, triggering dark rumors in Washington that he and his subordinates did not want to smite the enemy.

Confederate President Jefferson Davis suffered through a similarly trying period with Joseph Johnston. The two men quarrelled bitterly after Johnston learned in September 1861 that he would be the fourth-ranking full general in the Confederacy. Johnston insisted that he should be the

Confederacy's senior commander, engaging in an acrimonious correspondence that highlighted pettiness on both his and Davis's parts. During the ensuing months, Johnston, like McClellan, constantly requested more men and sniped at his civilian superiors.

A diplomatic crisis erupted as Lincoln and Davis labored to manage their principal commanders in Virginia. On November 8, Captain Charles Wilkes of the USS *San Jacinto* stopped the British vessel *Trent* and removed James Mason and John Slidell, a pair of Confederate diplomats bound for London and Paris respectively. The northern public lauded Wilkes's action, but the British government issued a strongly worded protest to the United States, demanded an apology and took steps to strengthen its military presence in Canada and the North Atlantic. After several tense weeks, during which Lincoln sought to find a graceful way to defuse the issue, the United States freed Mason and Slidell to travel to their original destinations. Anglo-American diplomatic relations had survived an initial stressful test.

The winter of 1861–62 passed without significant action in Virginia. McClellan devised a plan to turn Johnston's flank by moving his army by ship to the Rappahannock river and taking Fredericksburg. That would isolate Johnston in northern Virginia, forcing him to attack McClellan in order to reach Richmond. McClellan tarried, however, and a frustrated Lincoln finally ordered him to commence his campaign on February 22, 1862—George Washington's birthday. When that date came and went without a movement and the first days of March slipped by, Lincoln ended McClellan's stint as General-in-Chief.

Shenandoah valley campaign

Now just commander of the Army of the Potomac, Little Mac changed his plans when word arrived that Johnston had retreated to the Rappahannock line. On March 17, the Army of the Potomac began a larger turning movement towards Fort Monroe, situated at the tip of the finger of land between the York and James rivers known as the Peninsula. By the end of April, Confederate planners faced a range of threats in Virginia: the bulk of the Army of the Potomac lay on the lower Peninsula; another 30,000 Federals under Irvin McDowell near Fredericksburg; 15,000 under Nathaniel P. Banks in the lower Shenandoah valley, and nearly 10,000 under John C. Frémont in the Allegheny Mountains west of the valley.

The Confederates responded by concentrating forces near Richmond and mounting a diversion in the Shenandoah valley. Johnston fell back to the Peninsula, where he contested a slow Union advance towards the capital. As the forces under

Johnston and McClellan sought to gain an advantage over each other, the ironclad CSS *Virginia* (popularly called the "Merrimac') was scuttled on May 11. The *Virginia* had raised hopes in many a Confederate breast after its historic victories over several wooden warships on March 8, before fighting the Union ironclad USS *Monitor* to a draw at Hampton Roads the next day. "No one event of the war," remarked Confederate ordnance chief Josiah Gorgas from his post in Richmond, "created such a profound sensation as the destruction of this noble ship." Heavy rains drenched the Peninsula during May, adding to Confederate gloom over the *Virginia* and affording McClellan a good excuse for making little headway. The end of the month found the two forces—more than 100,000 Federals and about 70,000 Confederates—arrayed opposite one another along the Chickahominy river just east of Richmond.

By that time, the first major southern response to McClellan's Peninsula offensive had come in the Shenandoah valley. General Robert E. Lee, acting as principal military adviser to Jefferson Davis, proposed to reinforce Stonewall Jackson's small force in the valley with Richard S. Ewell's division, bringing it to about 17,500 men. He wished for Jackson to pin down all the troops belonging to Banks and Frémont so that they could not join in the advance against Richmond. Jackson had gained attention with an offensive movement in late March that resulted in a sharp action at First Kernstown. Although a tactical defeat, that fight had prompted the Federals to hold Banks and Frémont in the valley, which in turn set up Jackson's subsequent campaign.

Many civilians kept diaries that illuminate attitudes and morale on the respective home fronts. From her home in eastern North Carolina, Catherine Ann Devereux Edmondston drew on newspaper accounts, letters from friends and information gleaned from conversations to compile an exceptionally revealing diary. Like most Confederates, she preferred aggressive military leaders. First published in 1979, her diary merits the attention of anyone interested in the Confederacy. (Capital Area Preservation at Mordecai Historic Park, Raleigh, North Carolina)

Jackson stands as one of the most arresting military figures in United States history. Thirty-eight years old in May 1862, he was a devout Presbyterian of odd personal attitudes and characteristics. A British traveler in the Confederacy wrote in 1863, "I heard many anecdotes of the late 'Stonewall Jackson.' When he left the US service he was under the impression that one of his legs was shorter than the other; and afterwards his idea was that he only perspired on one side, and that it was necessary to keep the arm and leg of the other side in constant motion in order to preserve circulation." Secretive, stern and unyielding, Jackson took a very hard view of war. Above all, he fought aggressively, moved rapidly (his infantry became known as "foot cavalry') and pressed his soldiers to the limit in search of decisive victories.

The outline of Jackson's valley campaign may be sketched quickly. He took part of his force westwards from Staunton to strike the advance element of Frémont's force under Robert H. Milroy at McDowell on May 8, 1862. With these Federals retreating into the wilds of the western Virginia Alleghenies after a largely inconclusive engagement, Jackson hastened back to the valley. He then moved north towards New Market, while Ewell's division paralleled his march to the east in the Luray valley (the Massanutten Range divides the Shenandoah valley into western and eastern sections for 50 miles (80 km) between Harrisonburg on the south and Strasburg on the north; the Luray or Page valley constitutes the eastern portion of the valley). Crossing to the Luray valley at New Market Gap, Jackson joined Ewell and captured a Federal garrison at Front Royal on May 23, defeated Banks in the Battle of First Winchester on 25 May, and pursued retreating Federals all the way to the Potomac river.

Jackson had placed himself in an exposed position in the extreme northern reaches of the valley, and Federals planned a three-pronged offensive designed to cut him off north of Strasburg. Frémont would march east out of the Alleghenies, a division under James Shields would move west from Front Royal, and Banks would pursue southwards

from near Harpers Ferry. Jackson responded by driving his men to the limit. Aided by incredibly lethargic movement on the part of the Federals, he escaped the trap and marched southwards to the southern end of the Massanutten Range near Harrisonburg. There he turned on his pursuers, defeating Frémont at Cross Keys on June 8 and Shields at Port Republic on June 9.

In a whirlwind of action, Jackson's Army of the Valley had marched more than 350 miles (560 km), won a series of small battles, immobilized 60,000 Union troops, inflicted twice as many casualties as it suffered, and captured a great quantity of military supplies. After the twin victories on June 8–9, the Federals retreated northwards down the valley, and Jackson joined the Confederate forces defending Richmond.

Perhaps most important, Jackson's campaign inspirited a Confederate populace starved for good news from the battlefield. A North Carolina woman named Catherine Ann Devereux Edmondston wrote a typical reaction, in which she pointedly contrasted Jackson's accomplishment with Joseph Johnston's performance. "Jackson has gained another victory in the Valley of Va.," she wrote on June 11. "He has beaten Shields & holds Fremont in check, who fears to attack him singly. ... He is the only one of our generals who gives the enemy no rest, no time to entrench themselves. Matters before Richmond look gloomy to us out siders. McClellan advances, entrenching as he comes. Why do we allow it?'

The situation at Richmond did look serious for Confederates in early June. Relatively inactive during much of Jackson's valley campaign, the armies under McClellan and Johnston had fought their first major battle on May 31 and June 1 at Seven Pines (also called Fair Oaks). Johnston had retreated as far as he could without reaching the defensive works of Richmond. Faced with the prospect of a siege that would inevitably favor McClellan, he attacked on the 31st. Wretched coordination, a poor grasp of local terrain and other factors plagued the southern army in a battle that

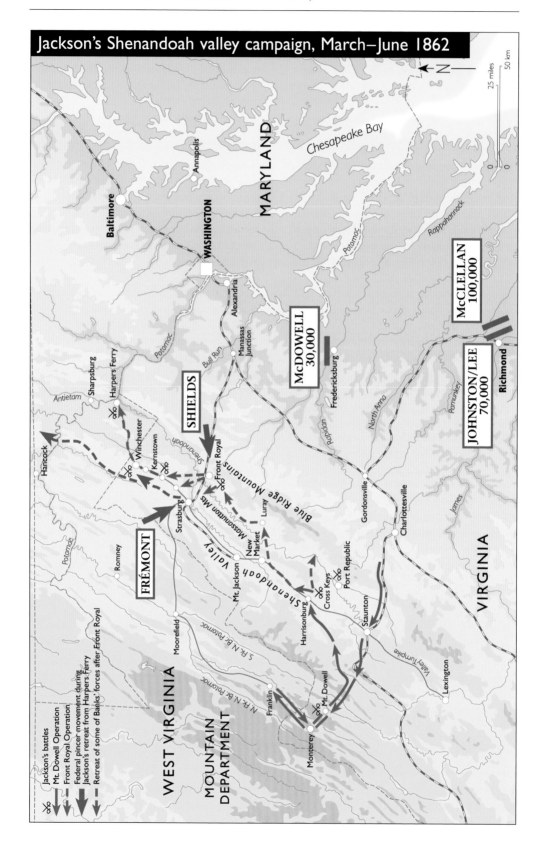

Jackson's Shenandoah valley campaign, March–June 1862

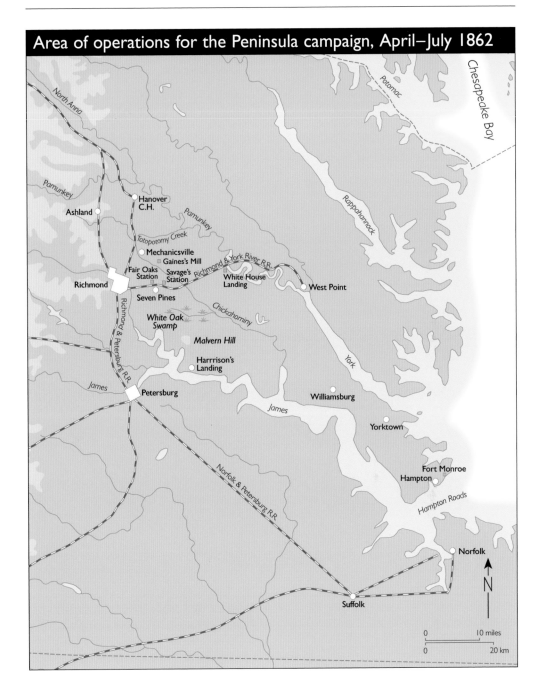

Area of operations for the Peninsula campaign, April–July 1862

Chesapeake Bay

Potomac

North Anna

Pamunkey

Ashland

Hanover C.H.

Pamunkey

Totopotomy Creek

Mechanicsville

Gaines's Mill

Fair Oaks Station

Savage's Station

Richmond & York River R.R.

White House Landing

Richmond

Seven Pines

West Point

White Oak Swamp

Chickahominy

Richmond & Petersburg R.R.

Malvern Hill

Harrrison's Landing

York

James

Petersburg

Williamsburg

James

Yorktown

Norfolk & Petersburg R.R.

Fort Monroe

Hampton

Hampton Roads

Norfolk

N

Suffolk

Rappahannock

0   10 miles

0   20 km

ended in tactical stalemate. More than 6,000 Confederates and 5,000 Federals fell in the two days, most notably Johnston, who suffered a severe wound in the chest. On June 1, Jefferson Davis named Robert E. Lee to succeed Johnston. Thus did the man who would become the greatest Confederate general step into the limelight.

Lee possessed impeccable credentials. Fifty-five years old, he belonged to one of the nation's first families and had compiled an exceptional record at West Point, as an engineer in the antebellum years and as a member of Winfield Scott's staff in Mexico. Superintendent at West Point for several years in the 1850s, Lee followed his native

Robert Edward Lee in 1862. A robust man with dark hair and moustache in May 1861, Lee grew a beard that quickly turned gray and then almost white. Just before the Seven Days, a member of Jefferson Davis's staff disagreed with those who considered Lee timid, describing him as the "one man in either army, Federal or Confederate, who is, head & shoulders, far above every other one in either army in audacity. … Lee is audacity personified." (Author's collection)

Virginia out of the Union in April 1861. He began the war as a figure from whom much was expected, before plummeting in the public's estimation following his activities in western Virginia and along the South Atlantic coast during the autumn and winter of 1861–62—service that lacked what the Confederate people considered a suitable offensive component. Diarist Catherine Edmondston responded unfavorably to reports of Lee's assuming command of the army after Seven Pines. In words echoed in many quarters across the Confederacy, Edmondston stated, "I do not much like him, he 'falls back' too much. He failed in Western Va owing, it was said, to the weather, has done little in the eyes of outsiders in S C. His nick name last summer was 'old-stick-in-the-mud' … pray God he may not fulfil the whole of his name."

Armistead L. Long, who served on Lee's staff during the war, recalled the winter of 1861–62 as a time when the press and public were "clamorous" against his superior, and Edward Porter Alexander, another staff member in June 1862, remembered that when Lee assumed command "some of the newspapers—particularly the Richmond *Examiner*—pitched into him with extraordinary virulence," insisting that "henceforth our army would never be allowed to fight."

The Seven Days battles

The next five weeks proved Lee's critics wrong. No general exhibited more daring than the new southern commander, who believed the Confederacy could counter northern numbers only by seizing and holding the initiative. He spent June preparing for a supreme effort against McClellan. When Jackson's valley troops and other reinforcements arrived, Lee's army, at 90,000 strong, would be the largest ever fielded by the South. By the last week of June, the Army of the Potomac lay astride the Chickahominy, two-thirds south of the river and one-third north of it. Lee hoped to crush the portion north of the river then turn against the rest. Confederates repulsed a strong Union reconnaissance against their left on June 25, opening what became known as the Seven Days battles and setting the stage for Lee's offensive.

Heavy fighting began on June 26, 1862 at the Battle of Mechanicsville and continued for the next five days. Lee consistently acted as the aggressor, but never managed to land a decisive blow. At Mechanicsville, he expected Jackson to strike Union General Fitz John Porter's right flank. The hero of the valley failed to appear in time, however, and A. P. Hill's Confederate division launched a futile frontal assault about mid-afternoon. Porter retreated to a strong position at Gaines's Mill, where Lee attacked again on the 27th. Once again Jackson stumbled, as more than 50,000 Confederates mounted

Fitz John Porter, whose 5th Corps bore the brunt of Union fighting at Mechanicsville, Gaines's Mill and Malvern Hill. A conservative Democrat and supporter of McClellan, Porter attracted the ire of congressional Republicans. Court-martialed for his role in the Second Bull Run campaign, he was stripped of command and dismissed from the army in January 1863. Sixteen years later, a military board cleared him of all charges. (Author's collection)

savage attacks along a wide front. Late in the day, John Bell Hood's Texas Brigade spearheaded an effort that broke Porter's lines and pushed the Federals across the Chickahominy to rejoin the bulk of McClellan's army. Jackson's poor performance, most often attributed to exhaustion verging on numbness, joined poor staff work and other factors in allowing Porter's exposed portion of McClellan's army to escape.

In the wake of Gaines's Mill, McClellan changed his base from the Pamunkey river to the James river, where northern naval power could support the Army of the Potomac. Lee followed the retreating McClellan, who insisted that the rebels badly outnumbered his army. He sought to inflict a crippling blow as the Federals retreated southward across the Peninsula. After heavy skirmishing on June 28, the Confederates launched

ineffectual attacks on the 29th at Savage's Station and far heavier ones at Glendale (also known as Frayser's Farm) on the 30th. Stonewall Jackson played virtually no role in these actions, as time and again the Confederates failed to act in concert.

By July 1, McClellan stood at Malvern Hill, a splendid defensive position overlooking the James. Lee resorted to unimaginative frontal assaults that afternoon. Whether driven by vexation at lost opportunities or his natural combativeness, he had made one of his

poorest tactical decisions. Southern division commander Daniel Harvey Hill said of the action on July 1, "It was not war, it was murder." As evening fell, more than 5,000 Confederate casualties littered the slopes of Malvern Hill. Some of McClellan's

The Confederate attacks at Gaines's Mill involved roughly 50,000 men, dwarfing in size the far more famous Pickett–Pettigrew assault at Gettysburg on July 3, 1863. In this crude post-war engraving, the artist attempted to suggest the magnitude and fury of the attacks. (Author's collection)

officers urged a counterattack against the obviously battered enemy; however, Little Mac retreated down the James to Harrison's Landing, where he awaited Lee's next move and issued endless requests for more men and supplies.

Casualties for the entire Peninsula campaign exceeded 50,000, more than 36,000 of whom had fallen during the Seven Days. Lee's losses from Mechanicsville to Malvern Hill exceeded 20,000 killed, wounded and missing, while McClellan's surpassed 16,000. Gaines's Mill, where combined losses exceeded 15,000, marked the point of greatest slaughter. Thousands of dead and maimed soldiers brought the reality of war to Richmond's residents. One woman wrote that "death held a carnival in our city. The weather was excessively hot. It was midsummer, gangrene and erysipelas attacked the wounded, and those who might have been cured of their wounds were cut down by these diseases."

The campaign's importance extended far beyond setting a new standard of carnage in Virginia. Lee had seized the initiative, dramatically altering the strategic picture by dictating the action to a compliant McClellan. Lee's first effort in field command lacked tactical polish, but nevertheless generated immense dividends. The Seven Days saved Richmond and inspirited a Confederate people buffeted by dismal military news from other theaters. On the Union side, the campaign dampened expectations of victory that had mounted steadily as northern armies in Tennessee and along the Mississippi river won a string of successes. McClellan's failure also exacerbated northern political divisions, clearing the way for Republicans to implement harsher policies that would strike at slavery and other rebel property. The end of the rebellion had seemed to be in sight when McClellan prepared to march up the Peninsula; after Malvern Hill, only the most obtuse observers failed to see that the war would continue in a more all-encompassing manner. "We have been and are in a depressed, dismal, asthenic state of anxiety and irritability," wrote a

Major-General John Pope, whose orders and public statements in Virginia during the summer of 1862 made Confederates savor his defeat at Second Bull Run. "The old army officers now among the Confederates," wrote one of Lee's artillerists after the war, "used to smile to think how Pope had managed to impose himself upon Mr Lincoln." (Author's collection)

perceptive New Yorker after McClellan's retreat. "The cause of the country does not seem to be thriving just now."

The campaign underscored the degree to which events in the Virginia theater dominated perceptions about the war's progress. Despite enormous northern achievement in the western campaigns, most people North and South, as well as observers in Britain and France, looked to Virginia. Lincoln spoke to this phenomenon in a famous letter to a French diplomat in early August, complaining that "it seems unreasonable that a series of successes, extending through half-a-year, and clearing more than a hundred thousand square miles of country, should help us so little, while a single half-defeat should hurt us so much." Lincoln did not exaggerate the impact of McClellan's failure. However, taken overall, the ramifications were such that the

Richmond campaign must be reckoned one of the turning points of the war.

Yet victory in the Seven Days battles had not removed the Union threat from Virginia. McClellan's host remained just a few miles below Richmond, and Major-General John Pope commanded the newly consolidated troops of Frémont, Banks, and McDowell in north-central Virginia. Denominated the Army of Virginia, Pope's force could operate against the railroads between Warrenton and Gordonsville, thus endangering the flow of supplies from the Shenandoah valley to Richmond and imperiling Lee's western flank.

Pope descended from a prominent family in Kentucky, had collateral ties to George Washington and was connected by marriage to Mrs Lincoln's family. A West Pointer and veteran of the war with Mexico, he had won victories along the Mississippi river earlier in 1862. Unlike most senior officers in McClellan's army, Pope agreed with Republicans who sought to wage a tougher war against the rebels. Pope promised to hang guerrillas, arrest citizens who aided them, confiscate all rebel property, and displace civilians who would not take the oath of allegiance to the United States. Although he neither engaged in mass hangings nor drove many people from their homes, his soldiers did seize or destroy an enormous amount of property. Pope also manifested personal arrogance in issuing several bombastic statements about how he would thrash Lee's army. His actions and pronouncements earned the enmity of white southerners and provoked Lee to write in late July that he hoped to destroy "the miscreant Pope."

Pope rather than McClellan emerged as Lee's principal Union opponent in the next campaign. This stemmed partly from Lee's and Jefferson Davis's determination to protect their fragile rail links to the Shenandoah valley. But McClellan's behavior also figured in the equation. Little Mac showed no inclination to resume active operations against Richmond, preferring to whine about reinforcements and lecture Lincoln on the need to refrain from seizing

rebel property or forcing emancipation on the South. A visit to McClellan's headquarters at Harrison's Landing on July 8–9 convinced Lincoln that he could expect no aggressive action in that arena. Later that month, McClellan received orders to leave the Peninsula and unite in northern Virginia with Pope's 55,000 men.

Lee kept an eye on both Pope and McClellan throughout a tense July. During this period, he reorganized his Army of Northern Virginia, dividing the infantry into two wings commanded by Stonewall Jackson and Major-General James Longstreet. He sent Jackson and 24,000 troops to Gordonsville during July, granting his lieutenant wide latitude in responding to any movement from Pope. On 9 August, Jackson defeated part of the Army of Virginia in the Battle of Cedar Mountain, fought north of Culpeper between the Rapidan and Rappahannock rivers. Shortly thereafter, having decided that McClellan was withdrawing from the Peninsula, Lee ordered Longstreet's wing to join Jackson's near Gordonsville. The Confederate chieftain hoped to defeat the Army of Virginia before it could unite with McClellan's Army of the Potomac. A period of maneuvering and probing along the Rappahannock river ensued, during which Lee and Pope sought to catch each other off guard.

Battle of Second Manassas or Bull Run

Lee took control of the campaign in late August 1862 when he ordered Jackson to make a sweeping march around Pope's right flank. On August 25–27, Jackson's infantry covered 56 miles (90 km) in brutal heat and captured Pope's massive supply base at Manassas Junction. Lee's army now offered a tempting target, with its two main pieces separated by Pope's army. Pope reacted to the threat in his rear by concentrating against Jackson, who formed a defensive line near the Warrenton Turnpike on the battlefield of First Manassas. The initial clash of the Battle of Second Manassas or Bull Run took place on August 28 at the Brawner Farm. There the Stonewall Brigade and the Union's Iron Brigade engaged in a famous stand-up fight at a distance of less than 100 yards (92m). A series of Union assaults the next day pressed Jackson's defenders, whose line ran along an unfinished railroad bed, to the limit. More than once the attackers broke through, only to be driven back by reinforcements. In the course of the long day's action, Jackson grimly told A. P. Hill, "If you are attacked again, you will beat the enemy back."

While Jackson's troops tenaciously held their ground, Lee and Longstreet arrived with the rest of the Army of Northern Virginia. Longstreet's left joined Jackson's right, and by about noon the whole line approximated an open V—Jackson's men facing generally south-east and Longstreet's nearly due east. Lee initially wanted Longstreet to attack, but consented to postponements when intelligence suggested a Union movement towards the southern right. Other than a brief clash at about 7 PM, Longstreet's soldiers remained inactive on the 29th.

Pope planned additional attacks against Jackson on August 30. Despite the protestations of Fitz John Porter and others, he clung to the idea that Longstreet's wing had not reached the field and insisted that a final push would drive Jackson away. After a series of delays, the Federals advanced at about 3 PM. Jackson's weary soldiers, ably supported by southern artillery that fired directly into the Union flank, repulsed the attackers. At about 4 PM, Longstreet launched a spectacular counterstroke that yielded a second stunning Confederate success at Manassas. Tenacious Union units, some of them fighting on Henry Hill, helped slow Longstreet's attackers long enough for Pope to organize an effective withdrawal. One Confederate soldier graphically described firing at a group of retreating Federals "so near and so thick" that "every shot took effect. ... We shot into this mass as fast as we could load until our guns got so hot we had at times to wait for them to cool." A few days after the battle, a Union survivor described his experience amid the chaos of Longstreet's attack. "I saw the men dropping on all sides," he wrote, "canteens struck and flying to pieces, haversacks cut off, rifles knocked to pieces, it was a perfect hail of bullets. I was expecting to get it every second, but on, on, I went, the balls hissing by my head."

Pope withdrew to Washington in good order, blocking a Confederate blow at Chantilly on September 1 and reaching the city's formidable entrenchments the next day. His successful escape did little to soften the impact of another Federal defeat. The campaign had cost Pope 16,000 casualties out of approximately 75,000 engaged (some units from the Army of the Potomac had reinforced the Army of Virginia). Lee lost about 9,200 out of 50,000 engaged. Lee's bold decision to split his army, swift marching and hard fighting had paid off for the Confederates. Pope had proved to be aggressive but inept, and Lincoln removed him from command on September 2. For the second time in 13 months, George B. McClellan stepped forward to restore order following a northern defeat in Virginia.

Lee lost little time in preparing his next movement. He had accomplished a remarkable strategic reorientation in Virginia, shifting the military frontier from Richmond to the banks of the Potomac river. Seeking to maintain the strategic initiative and improve his logistical situation, he decided to take the war across the Potomac into the United States. He knew the Army of Northern Virginia had suffered enormously during the preceding ten weeks. As one veteran wrote, by early September the army's "divisions had sunk to little more than brigades, & brigades nearly to regiments." Indeed, the average southern regiment would number fewer than 175 men during the upcoming campaign. Still, Lee wrote to Jefferson Davis on September 3 that he considered it "to be the most propitious time since the commencement of the war for the Confederate Army to enter Maryland."

Several factors influenced Lee. Logistically, he wanted to collect food and forage in Maryland and Pennsylvania, remaining north long enough to allow Virginia farmers

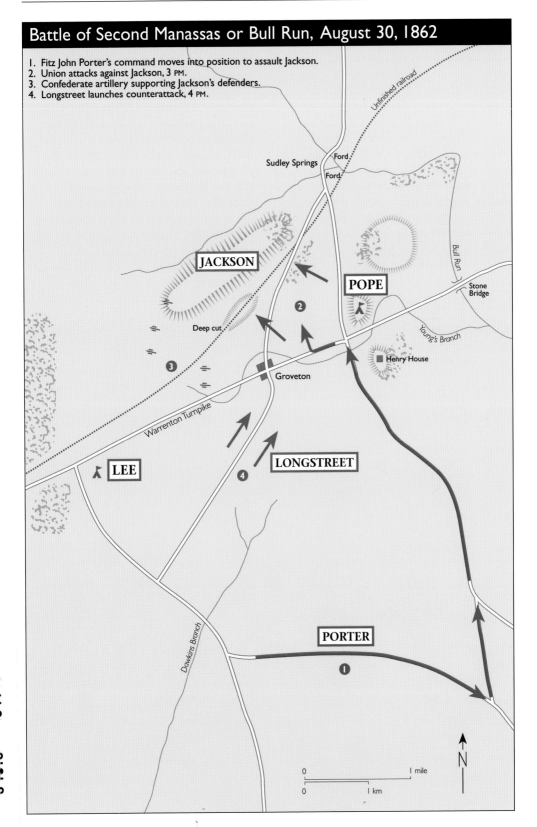

Battle of Second Manassas or Bull Run, August 30, 1862

1. Fitz John Porter's command moves into position to assault Jackson.
2. Union attacks against Jackson, 3 PM.
3. Confederate artillery supporting Jackson's defenders.
4. Longstreet launches counterattack, 4 PM.

Unfinished railroad

Sudley Springs   Ford
Ford

JACKSON

POPE

Bull Run

Stone
Bridge

Deep cut

Young's Branch

Henry House

Groveton

Warrenton Turnpike

LEE

LONGSTREET

Dawkins Branch

PORTER

0   1 mile

0   1 km

N

to gather their autumn harvest. The enemy would have to follow him into Maryland, thus sparing Richmond from a fresh Federal advance. His presence above the Potomac during the North's autumn elections also might hurt the Republicans and bolster advocates of peace. Moreover, if he stayed north until late autumn, he might forestall another Union offensive in Virginia until the spring of 1863. Finally, his army's presence might inspire slaveholding Marylanders to flock to the Confederate colors. Although Lee did not expect help from abroad, a victory north of the Potomac could prove decisive in persuading leaders in London and Paris to extend formal recognition to the Confederacy. Prime Minister Palmerston had

interpreted the Seven Days as evidence of impending Confederate success, suggesting to the Queen on August 6 that Britain consider proposing an armistice in October.

The Army of Northern Virginia began crossing the Potomac on September 4, 1862, and events unfolded rapidly over the next two weeks. Lee divided his army while at Frederick, Maryland, on September 9. He assigned the majority of it to Stonewall Jackson, who was to capture Harpers Ferry (control of that point would give Lee a secure supply line to the lower Shenandoah valley) while Longstreet and the rest of the army marched towards Hagerstown. McClellan had followed cautiously. Lincoln saw Lee's invasion as an opportunity to

punish the rebels. On September 12, his greatest fear was that the rebels would escape to Virginia unscathed. Late that afternoon the President urged McClellan not to let Lee "get off without being hurt."

The next day, in an incredible stroke of luck, Union soldiers rummaging through abandoned Confederate camps at Frederick found a copy of Lee's operational blueprint. The document quickly made its way to Union headquarters, where McClellan instantly grasped its importance. Turning to a subordinate, he said, "Here is a paper with which if I cannot whip Bobbie Lee, I will be willing to go home." But precious hours ticked by before the Federal chief bestirred himself to press the invaders. While Jackson

laid siege to Harpers Ferry on September 14, McClellan's troops forced Lee's defenders out of the gaps of South Mountain in sharp fighting. Lee briefly thought about abandoning Maryland, then decided to concentrate his army near Sharpsburg. Two days passed with little action on Lee's and McClellan's front, but Harpers Ferry and its 12,000-man garrison surrendered on the 15th, freeing Jackson to hasten to Lee's support.

James Longstreet committed nearly 30,000 Confederates to his impressive counterattack against the Army of Virginia on the afternoon of August 30. His wing lost more men in a few hours of hard combat than Jackson's had in three days of fighting. This post-war painting shows Union officers trying to form a line of battle to stem the Confederate tide. (Author's collection)

Battle of Antietam
or Sharpsburg

The climactic clash came on September 17 at the Battle of Antietam (called Sharpsburg by most Confederates). Straggling and desertion had reduced Lee's army to fewer than 40,000 men. McClellan's army numbered more than 80,000, though a quarter had been in service only a few weeks. The battle unfolded from north to south in three distinct phases. Between about 6 and 9:30 AM, Federals from three corps pounded the Confederate left under Stonewall Jackson. Lee shifted troops from his right, commanded by Longstreet, to shore up his harried left. Particularly vicious action occurred in a 23-acre (9.3 ha) cornfield owned by a farmer named David R. Miller. Some 8,000 men, including more than 80 percent of one Texas regiment, fell in the midst of cornstalks cut down by musketry and cannon fire. This part of the fighting ended with the near destruction of a Union division that stumbled into a deadly crossfire in woods near a modest brick church that served a Dunker congregation.

Lee's invasion of Maryland represented the final act in a three-part drama that opened at the Seven Days, continued with the Battle of Second Manassas and closed with the fearful slaughter at Antietam. The entire campaign from June to September dramatically reoriented the war in the Eastern Theater. *Harper's Weekly* depicted Confederates crossing the Potomac into Maryland on a brightly moonlit night. (Author's collection)

The second phase focused on the middle of Lee's position and lasted from 9:30 AM until about 1 PM. Two Confederate brigades situated in a sunken country lane held this section of the line. Together with other units that came to their aid, these brigades beat back a series of Union attacks before being flanked and driven out at great loss. Lee had no reinforcements at hand, and his army teetered on the edge of utter defeat. Union division commander Israel Richardson, whose soldiers had broken the rebel line, pleaded with McClellan to send in reinforcements. Thousands of uncommitted Federals stood nearby, but McClellan chose not to send them forward lest he leave himself without a substantial reserve. A staggering opportunity slipped away as action died down along what the soldiers later christened the "Bloody Lane."

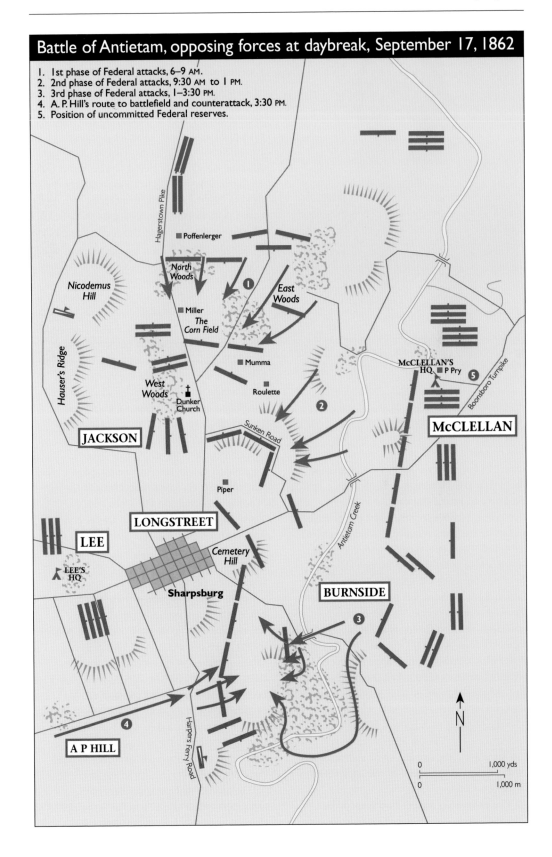

Battle of Antietam, opposing forces at daybreak, September 17, 1862

1. 1st phase of Federal attacks, 6–9 AM.
2. 2nd phase of Federal attacks, 9:30 AM to 1 PM.
3. 3rd phase of Federal attacks, 1–3:30 PM.
4. A. P. Hill's route to battlefield and counterattack, 3:30 PM.
5. Position of uncommitted Federal reserves.

Hagerstown Pike

Poffenlerger

North Woods

East Woods

Nicodemus Hill

Miller
The Corn Field

Hauser's Ridge

Mumma

McCLELLAN'S HQ P Pry

Boonsboro Turnpike

West Woods

Roulette

Dunker Church

JACKSON

Sunken Road

McCLELLAN

Piper

LONGSTREET

Cemetery Hill

Antietam Creek

LEE

LEE'S HQ

Sharpsburg

BURNSIDE

N

A P HILL

Harpers Ferry Road

| 0 | 1,000 yds |
| 0 | 1,000 m |

Major-General Ambrose Powell Hill, whose "Light Division" played a major role in all of the Army of Northern Virginia's battles in 1862–63. About two weeks after Antietam, Lee praised Hill highly in a letter to Jefferson Davis. Apart from Jackson and Longstreet, wrote Lee, "I consider A. P. Hill the best commander with me. He fights his troops well, and takes good care of them." (Author's collection)

The battle closed on the Confederate right, where Major-General Ambrose E. Burnside orchestrated an unimpressive tactical offensive against a handful of southern defenders. Fighting on this part of the field began just as the action in the Sunken Road subsided. Two Federal regiments crossed a stone bridge over Antietam Creek (later dubbed "Burnside's Bridge') under fire, after which Burnside took his time preparing for a final advance. If successful, Burnside's soldiers could cut Lee and his army off from the only available ford over the Potomac. By about 3 PM, Union attackers had approached to within 250 yards (230 m) of the road to the ford when elements of A. P. Hill's division slammed into their left flank. A difficult 17-mile (27 km) march from Harpers Ferry had carried Hill's leading brigades to the field just in time to disrupt Burnside's attacks. The battle closed as the Federals fell back towards Antietam Creek.

The exhausted armies had waged the costliest single day's combat in United States history. McClellan's loss approached 12,500, and Lee's exceeded 10,300. Another 2,300 Federals and 2,700 Confederates had fallen at South Mountain on September 14. One southerner remarked that the "sun seemed almost to go backwards" during the fighting on the 17th. A Union soldier counted himself fortunate that his regiment did not have to view the shattered landscape in full daylight. "We were glad to march over the field at night," he told his parents, "for we could not see the horrible sights so well. Oh what a smell[,] some of the men vomit as they went along."

The Army of Northern Virginia remained on the field during September 18, after which McClellan permitted Lee to recross the Potomac unmolested. A Federal foray across the river at Shepherdstown late on the 19th promised to disrupt Lee's withdrawal, but A. P. Hill's division counterattacked the following day and drove the northerners back to the left bank of the Potomac. The campaign closed without a determined Union effort to pursue the Confederates.

McClellan's handling of the campaign inspired heated debate. While some applauded his success in stopping Lee's invasion, others inside the Army of the Potomac and behind the lines in the North believed he had lost a tantalizing opportunity. A newspaper correspondent voiced a common criticism in wishing McClellan had attacked again on September 18: "We could have driven them into the river or captured them. ... It was one of the supreme moments when by daring something, the destiny of the nation might have been changed." No one experienced more bitter disappointment than Abraham Lincoln. Although he used Lee's retreat as a pretext to issue a preliminary Emancipation Proclamation on September 22, a step that signalled a profound shift in the course of the war, he nevertheless believed his commander had once again shown insufficient aggressiveness.

Thousands of Union soldiers had remained out of the action on September 17 (Lee, in contrast, had committed every available man) and reinforcements had reached the field on the 18th, yet still McClellan refused to advance. He insisted that his men were worn out, too few in number to harass the rebels, and poorly supplied. Secretary of the Navy Gideon Welles likely mirrored Lincoln's attitude when he wrote on September 19 that he had no news from the army, "except that, instead of following up the victory, attacking and capturing the Rebels," McClellan was allowing Lee to escape across the Potomac. An obviously unhappy Welles added: "McClellan says they are crossing, and that Pleasonton is after them. Oh dear!'

McClellan typically lavished praise on himself. "I feel some little pride," he wrote to his wife on September 20, "in having, with a beaten and demoralised army, defeated Lee so utterly and saved the North so completely. Well—one of these days history will I trust do me justice in deciding that it was not my

fault that the campaign of the Peninsula was not successful." The next day he complained that Lincoln and the Secretary of War had not congratulated him sufficiently. But he assured his wife that a higher power had blessed his work: "I have the satisfaction of knowing that God has in His mercy a second time made me the instrument for saving the nation & am content with the honor that has fallen to my lot."

If McClellan erred on the side of caution in September 1862, Robert E. Lee might have

Northern photographers reached the battlefield at Antietam before the Confederate dead had been buried. Their studies of southern corpses created a sensation in the North. An article in the *New York Times* remarked that the photographs "bring home to us the terrible reality and earnestness of war." The pictures did not lay bodies "in our door-yards and along streets" but accomplished "something very like it." This view shows Confederates, most likely from William E. Starke's Louisiana brigade, along the Hagerstown Pike. (Author's collection)

Lincoln visited the Army of the Potomac in early October, hoping to prod McClellan into advancing against Lee's army. As he and a companion looked over the army's headquarters camp one morning, Lincoln asked the man what he saw. The Army of the Potomac, came the answer. "No, you are mistaken," said Lincoln, "that is General McClellan's bodyguard." In this photograph, Lincoln and McClellan sit stiffly in the General's field tent. (Library of Congress)

been too audacious. Thousands of Confederates had fallen at Antietam when Lee stood to gain very little either tactically or strategically. The decision to remain on the field on the 18th, with a powerful enemy in his front and just a single ford available to reach Virginia, might have jeopardized his entire army. He had driven his worn army relentlessly, misjudging the men's physical capacity and watching thousands fall out of the ranks from hunger, debility or a simple unwillingness to be pushed any further. The army had survived, however, and as it lay in camps near Winchester, Lee congratulated the soldiers who had discharged their duty. History offered "few examples of greater fortitude and endurance than this army has exhibited," he assured them, "to your tried valor and patriotism the country looks with confidence for deliverance and safety."

Lee did not exaggerate how important his soldiers' activities would be to future Confederate morale. No one could claim a clear-cut success for the army. Marylanders had not rushed to the Confederate colors, and the army fell back to Virginia long before Lee had expected. Yet he had accomplished many of his logistical goals by virtue of McClellan's failure to press him after September 17. More significantly, between June and September 1862, the Army of Northern Virginia had crafted spectacular victories that helped cancel the effects of defeats in other theaters. The retreat from Maryland, itself counterbalanced by the capture of thousands of Federals at Harpers Ferry and the tidy success at Shepherdstown, did not detract appreciably from laurels won at Richmond and Second Manassas. Similarly, the bitter contest at Sharpsburg, seen by most Confederates as a bloody drawn battle, confirmed the gallantry of Lee's soldiers. In the space of less than three months, the Confederate people had come to expect good news from Lee and the Army of Northern Virginia, investing ever more emotional capital in them. That investment led to a belief in possible victory that would be as important as any other factor in lengthening the life of the Confederacy.

Abraham Lincoln lost all patience with McClellan in the wake of Antietam. The outspoken general reiterated his opposition to emancipation, angering Republican politicians already eager to see him relieved. The principal problem from Lincoln's standpoint lay in McClellan's refusal to mount a new campaign into Virginia. In mid-October, an exasperated Lincoln asked whether his general was "over-cautious when you assume that you can not do what the enemy is constantly doing? Should you not claim to be at least his equal in prowess, and act upon the claim?" McClellan finally began crossing the Potomac on October 26. His army took six days to make the passage (Lee's had done it in one night after Antietam) and then marched slowly towards Warrenton. Nearly seven weeks had elapsed since Lee's retreat, and Lincoln had reached his breaking point. On November 5, the day after the northern off-year elections (elections held in between presidential elections), Lincoln issued orders replacing McClellan with Ambrose E. Burnside. Little Mac received the orders late in the evening on November 7. He took an emotional leave from the army three days later, having played his final scene in the war's military drama.

Battle of Fredericksburg

Burnside doubted his capacity for high command. At 38 years old, he could look back on a largely unexceptional career. He graduated from West Point in 1847 and served a few uneventful years in the army before resigning to enter civilian life. Trying unsuccessfully to market a carbine he had designed while in military service, he later worked for the same railroad that employed his friend McClellan. In 1861, he led a brigade at First Bull Run before winning several victories along the North Carolina coast. Powerfully built and bald, he affected luxuriant whiskers that swept down the sides of his face and joined to form a bushy moustache—the famous "Burnside cut"

Ambrose Everett Burnside in a wartime engraving. Although primarily remembered for losing the Battle of Fredericksburg, Burnside had previously earned a favorable reputation for overseeing successful operations along the North Carolina coast that employed land and naval forces. In February 1862, a New York diarist wrote: "Burnside is pushing on, up Albemarle Sound, it would seem. Hurrah for Burnside!" (Author's collection)

(from which the word "sideburns" derived). Personally brave and widely popular, he lacked the intellectual ability of a great commander.

His government expected him to organize a campaign against Richmond before the end of the year. Burnside knew that Lee's army was divided, with Jackson's Second Corps in the Shenandoah valley and Longstreet's First Corps near Culpeper (the Confederates had replaced wings with corps after Antietam). He proposed marching his 130,000 soldiers from northern Virginia to Fredericksburg, seizing that important city and striking south along the Richmond, Fredericksburg and Potomac Railroad. Lincoln and Major-General Henry W. Halleck, who had earned a high reputation in the Western Theater and been named General-in-Chief after the Seven Days, approved Burnside's plan and recommended that he move quickly.

Federal shelling of Fredericksburg on December 11 damaged a number of buildings and left many streets littered with rubble. In this regard, the old colonial city at the falls of the Rappahannock river anticipated the fate of many other southern communities. Confederates deplored the shelling of civilian neighborhoods in Fredericksburg, to which Federals responded that Lee's army should not have fought from the cover of private residences. (Author's collection)

Burnside reached the eastern bank of the Rappahannock river opposite Fredericksburg on November 19, 1862, but he could not cross into the city because necessary pontoon bridges had not arrived. Several days passed, affording Lee time to hurry Longstreet's soldiers to high ground west and south of Fredericksburg. Jackson's corps followed in early December, extending Lee's position along the Rappahannock below Fredericksburg.

Jackson's presence foreclosed the option of a Union crossing downstream, so Burnside settled on several points near the city. On December 11, engineers oversaw construction of pontoons at two points opposite the city and one about a mile (1.6 km) downstream. Confederates resisted the two upper crossings, firing on the bridge builders from the shelter of houses and other structures. Union artillery bombarded the city, driving civilians into the countryside and destroying a number of buildings. A Confederate artillerist described the memorable scene:

The city, except its steeples, was still veiled in the mist which had settled in the valleys. Above it and in it incessantly showed the round white

*clouds of bursting shells, and out of its midst
there soon rose three or four columns of dense
black smoke from houses set on fire by the
explosions. The atmosphere was so perfectly
calm and still that the smoke rose vertically in
great pillars for several hundred feet before
spreading outward in black sheets. … the dark
blue masses of over 100,000 infantry in compact
columns, and numberless parks of white-topped
wagons and ambulances massed in orderly
ranks, all awaited the completion of the bridges.
The earth shook with the thunder of the guns,
and, high above all, a thousand feet in the air,
hung two immense balloons. The scene gave
impressive ideas of the disciplined power of a
great army, and of the vast resources of the
nation which had sent it forth.*

Union troops held the city by evening
and sacked it the next day.

Burnside's final plan called for a flanking
movement that would cut the Army of
Northern Virginia off from the direct routes
to Richmond. The Federal army had been
organized into three Grand Divisions of two
corps each, commanded by William Buel
Franklin (the left), Joseph Hooker (the
center), and Edwin V. Sumner (the right).
On December 13, Hooker would hold Lee's
attention in front of Fredericksburg while
Franklin worked his way around the enemy's
right near Hamilton's Crossing.

Lee did not complete his defensive
dispositions until the morning of the 13th,
when the last of Jackson's corps reached the
field from down the Rappahannock. The
75,000 men of the Army of Northern
Virginia stretched nearly 7 miles (11 km),
their left anchored on high ground
overlooking the Rappahannock and their
right near Hamilton's Crossing. Longstreet's
corps held the left, accounting for 5 miles (8
km) of the front, and Jackson's corps
presented a defense in depth along the
rightmost 2 miles (3.2 km) of the southern
front. Longstreet's men occupied several
hills, most notably Marye's Heights west of
the city. Jackson's infantry and artillery
enjoyed less commanding ground. Moreover,
Jackson's final line suffered from a

600-yard (550m) gap that ran through a
boggy area—a weakness the General had
noticed. In 1864, D. H. Hill described a ride
that he and Jackson had taken on the
morning of the 13th: "As we passed by a flat
boggy piece of ground the General said, 'the
enemy will attack at this point.'"

The battle opened on the Confederate
right. A mid-morning artillery duel included
a daring set of maneuvers by the youthful
Confederate Major John Pelham, whose
brilliant use of two guns held up George
G. Meade's division of Union infantry for an
hour. About 1 PM, Meade's Pennsylvanians
advanced across an open plain against
A. P. Hill's division. Some of the Federals
struck the gap in the Confederate line,
surging up a wooded hill to a second line of
infantry. A confused South Carolina brigadier
mistakenly thought the Federals to be
Confederates and ordered his men not to
fire. He fell mortally wounded, but two of
Jackson's divisions quickly stopped Meade's
progress. When Grand Division commander
Franklin failed to provide supports for
Meade's hard-pressed units, the Federals
glumly withdrew. A pair of Confederate
brigades pursued their retreating foe until
savaged by northern artillery. Lee witnessed
this counterattack from his headquarters on
Telegraph Hill. A nearby staff officer heard
the commanding general say to James
Longstreet in low tones, "It is well this is so
terrible! We should grow too fond of it!'

John Gibbon's Union division also
attacked Jackson's line, only to suffer the
same fate as Meade's. This commitment of
just a fraction of his Grand Division seemed
to satisfy Franklin. He suspended active
operations, having failed utterly to execute
Burnside's instructions to turn the
Confederate right.

The focus soon shifted to a series of
Union frontal assaults against Longstreet's
troops on Marye's Heights. The defenders
occupied a splendid position. Infantrymen
crowded behind a stone wall in a sunken
road at the foot of the hill. Other brigades
rested within easy supporting distance to
their right and left. Artillery crowned the

George Gordon Meade's division of Pennsylvanians achieved the only Federal offensive success at Fredericksburg. Shortly after the battle, Meade told his wife that his "men went in *beautifully*, carried everything before them, and drove the enemy for nearly half a mile" until, "finding themselves unsupported on either right or left," they "were checked and finally driven back." Meade subsequently commanded the Army of the Potomac longer than any other officer. (Author's collection)

high ground above them. Longstreet exhibited the easy confidence of a soldier convinced his enemy could do him no serious harm. Other Confederates shared his outlook. One artillerist assured Longstreet just before the battle that southern guns covered the approaches so thoroughly that "a chicken could not live on that field when we open on it."

Those words proved to be prophetic. Between noon and 6 PM, several waves of attackers deployed west of Fredericksburg and marched up the gentle rise towards Marye's Heights. Temperatures climbed into the mid-50s Fahrenheit (about 13°C) on an unseasonably warm winter afternoon. The nature of the ground prevented deployment of more than one brigade at a time, which resulted in the sickening spectacle of successive units matching grit and courage against an unforgiving wall of Confederate musketry and cannon fire. None of the attackers received more attention from later writers than the famed Irish Brigade of Winfield Scott Hancock's division, which lost more than 500 men in its attack. But others absorbed far more punishment, including John C. Caldwell's brigade, which followed the Irishmen into the maelstrom and suffered 900 casualties.

One of Longstreet's soldiers in the sunken road described the action four days after the battle. "We waited until they got within about 200 yards of us," observed this man, "& rose to our feet & poured volley after volley into their ranks which told a most deadening effect. ... another column & another & still another came to their support. But our well aimed shots were more than they could stand so about night they were compelled to give up the field covered with their dead." A northern soldier described the harrowing passage back down the hill towards Fredericksburg: "All the way down the slope to the edge of the town I saw my fellow-soldiers dropping on every side, in their effort to get out of the reach of the murderous fire from the Confederate infantry securely entrenched behind the long stone wall and the batteries on the

Battle of Fredericksburg, December 13, 1862

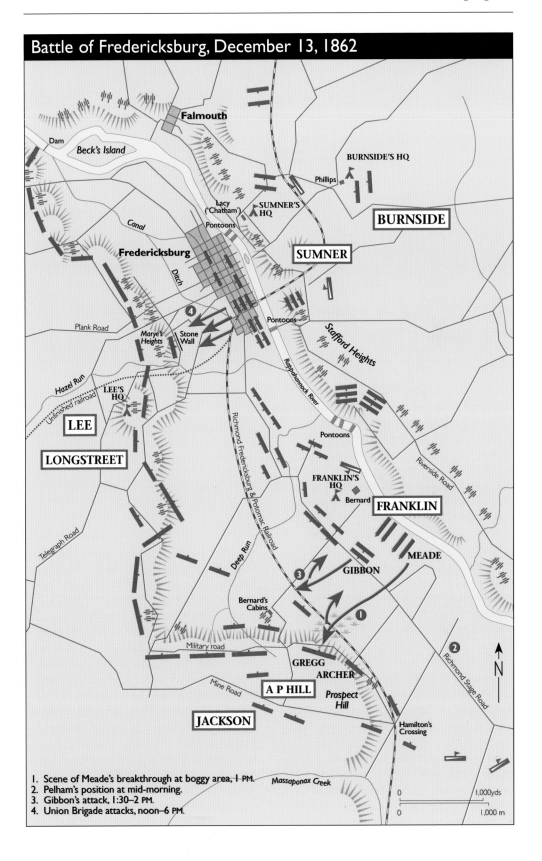

1. Scene of Meade's breakthrough at boggy area, I PM.
2. Pelham's position at mid-morning.
3. Gibbon's attack, 1:30–2 PM.
4. Union Brigade attacks, noon–6 PM.

heights." A union general observed simply that the area in front of Marye's Heights "was a great slaughter pen."

The Army of the Potomac remained in Fredericksburg and exchanged desultory fire with the Confederates for two more days. On the night of December 15, Burnside ordered a retreat across the river. A disappointed Lee, who had chafed at his inability to launch a counterattack because of Union batteries posted on high ground east of the Rappahannock, expressed disbelief that the enemy had given up the field without further struggle. The one-day battle had produced 12,650 Union casualties, most of whom had fallen in front of Marye's Heights. Most of the 5,300 Confederates who fell had been hit defending Jackson's position.

Burnside took full responsibility for the debacle and received fearful criticism from soldiers and civilians alike. Many in the North also assailed Lincoln as a failed war leader. The seemingly pointless, unimaginative nature of the attacks at Fredericksburg triggered especially bitter reactions. When first informed of what had happened on December 13, Lincoln told a friend, "If there is a worse place than Hell, I am in it."

Robert E. Lee and a group of staff officers and subordinates watch the Battle of Fredericksburg from atop Telegraph Hill (later called "Lee's Hill"). In this post-war engraving by Alfred A. Waud, James Longstreet is the fourth figure from the left. A witness on the hill described Longstreet, whom Lee had called "the staff in my right hand" after the Seven Days, as "about six feet, two inches high, a strong, round frame, portly and fleshy, but not corpulent or too fat." (Author's collection)

Confederates took heart from the easy victory. Their faith in Lee and his army deepened, prompting the General to worry lest they fall into the trap of believing the war was about to end. The enemy had "suffered heavily as far as the battle went," noted Lee, "but it did not go far enough to satisfy me … The contest will have now to be renewed, but on what field I cannot say."

Fighting in Virginia had ended for 1862, but Burnside's problems continued. An indifferent administrator, he presided over a dark period in his army's history. Morale plummeted and desertions increased. An attempted flanking movement around Lee's left, the infamous "Mud March," ground to an ignominious halt amid a spell of wet weather in January 1863. Many of Burnside's senior subordinates sought his removal.

Although unhappy with several of Burnside's critics in the army, Lincoln decided a change was needed. On January 26, Burnside relinquished command of the Army of the Potomac to Joseph Hooker, who became the army's third helmsman in just five months.

Another West Pointer with extensive experience during the war with Mexico, Hooker had left the army in the 1850s to live on the Pacific coast. He reentered the army shortly after the firing on Fort Sumter and proved to be a hard fighter. A press report from the Peninsula headed "Fighting—Joe Hooker" had mistakenly appeared in print as "Fighting Joe Hooker," thus bestowing a nickname that the General loathed. Hooker harbored enormous ambition and had lobbied behind the scenes to replace Burnside. A handsome 48-year-old bachelor when he took command of the army, he set up a convivial headquarters that offended many observers. Charles Francis Adams, Jr, the grandson of one president and great-grandson of another, scathingly described Hooker as a "noisy, low-toned intriguer under whose influence army headquarters became a place to which no

self-respecting man liked to go and no decent woman could go. It was a combination barroom and brothel." Lincoln knew about Hooker's machinations against Burnside as well as his intemperate comment that the nation might need a dictator to win the war. In a remarkable letter dated January 26, 1863, Lincoln listed Hooker's strengths and weaknesses as a man and officer. "Only those generals who gain successes, can set up dictators," stated Lincoln pointedly. "What I now ask of you is military success, and I will risk the dictatorship."

Hooker rapidly restored morale in the army. The quality of food and sanitation improved, desertions fell off, and Hooker instituted a system of corps badges that soon became prized symbols engendering pride in belonging to a particular corps. Hooker also

The Irish Brigade's performance at Fredericksburg figured prominently in post-war writings. Irish veterans used the valor displayed on December 13 to offset charges that overwhelmingly Democratic Irish Americans had not supported the Union. In this painting, soldiers in the 28th Massachusetts, one of five regiments in the brigade, advance up the slope towards Marye's Heights. (Osprey Publishing)

scrapped Burnside's Grand Divisions, preferring to work with individual corps commanders (seven Union corps would participate in the upcoming campaign). By the end of April, the Army of the Potomac represented a formidable military instrument. Its 134,000 well-equipped and supplied soldiers anticipated success. One Ohioan, impressed with the power of the army after a major review, remarked: "Such a great army! Thunder and lightning! The Johnnies could never whip this army!" Hooker described his force as "the finest army on the planet." A leading Confederate artillerist later agreed, writing of "Hooker's great army—the greatest this country had ever seen."

The Army of Northern Virginia lacked its opponent's size and material bounty, but

fully matched its confidence. A difficult winter had compelled Lee to disperse much of his cavalry to secure food for the horses. James Longstreet and two of his four infantry divisions had been detached to south-east Virginia, where they foraged on a grand scale and stood guard against possible Federal incursions from Norfolk and North Carolina. Scarcely more than

Outraged northerners echoed the feelings of a soldier who, with an indifferent grasp of spelling but a clear point of view, called Fredericksburg "The grates Slaughter or the Most Masterly pease of Boothchery that has hapend during the Ware and not a thing accomppehsed." Few images were more galling than that represented in this post-war engraving: well-protected Confederates behind a stone wall at the foot of Marye's Heights pouring musketry into the ranks of unseen charging Federals. (Author's collection)

Major-General Joseph Hooker, who predicted victory but refused to shoulder responsibility when his plans went awry. A Union artillerist heard Hooker try to shift blame for the defeat at Chancellorsville to 6th Corps commander John Sedgwick. "My feelings were divided between shame for my commanding general," remarked the artillerist in late May 1863, "and indignation at the attack on so true, brave, and modest a man as Sedgwick." (Author's collection)

60,000 Confederates of all arms prepared to defend the Rappahannock river lines. Yet most Confederates expected victory. They enjoyed superior generalship in the team of Lee and Jackson, who had forged remarkable bonds with their men and had an impressive record of victory. Dashing James Ewell Brown ("Jeb') Stuart supplied equally able leadership to the cavalry. The Army of Northern Virginia had often overcome intimidating odds to win victories, and its men believed their commanders would enable them to do so again. Stephen Dodson Ramseur, a youthful brigadier-general in Jackson's corps, reflected the army's confidence. The "vandal hordes of the Northern Tyrant are struck down with terror arising from their past experience," he stated. "They have learned to their sorrow that this army is made up of veterans equal to those of the 'Old Guard' of Napoleon."

Battle of Chancellorsville

The strategic initiative rested with Hooker, who developed an impressive plan. He proposed holding Lee's attention at Fredericksburg with about 40,000 men under John Sedgwick, while several corps made a rapid march up the Rappahannock to turn the rebel left and get in Lee's rear. Most of the army's cavalry would ride towards Richmond, cutting Lee's lines of communication with the Confederate capital. The turning column would have to move through an area south of the Rappahannock and Rapidan rivers known as the Wilderness of Spotsylvania, approximately 70 square miles (180 square kilometers) of scrub woods and tangled undergrowth that would retard effective deployment of Hooker's superior manpower and artillery. Once in Lee's rear, a fast march towards Fredericksburg would take the Federals out of the Wilderness into open ground, where their numbers would tell. If all went well, Lee's army would be trapped between the flanking column and Sedgwick's force at Fredericksburg.

The campaign began brilliantly for the Federals. On April 27, 1863, Hooker's turning column swung up the Rappahannock, negotiated fords over that river and the Rapidan, and by early afternoon on the 30th reached the crossroads of Chancellorsville some 10 miles (16 km) west of Fredericksburg. George G. Meade, who led the Union V Corps on the flanking maneuver, expressed unabashed enthusiasm at what Hooker had accomplished. "This is splendid," he said, "hurrah for old Joe; we are on Lee's flank, and he does not know it." A march of 2 or 3 miles (about 4 km) would take the Federals from Chancellorsville, which lay in the Wilderness, to clear ground farther east. But Hooker ordered the troops to remain at Chancellorsville, where he joined them that evening. The Federal commander announced to his army that "our enemy must either ingloriously fly, or come out from behind his defenses and give us battle on our own ground, where certain destruction awaits him." Lee reacted boldly to Hooker's maneuver. He divided his small army, leaving Jubal A. Early and about 10,000 men to watch Sedgwick at Fredericksburg and marching the other 50,000 to deal with the Federals at Chancellorsville. The critical moment of the campaign occurred on the morning of May 1. Hooker's advancing infantry clashed with Confederates 3.5 miles (5.6 km) east of Chancellorsville near Zoan Church, whereupon the Union commander ordered a withdrawal. Some of Hooker's subordinates argued vehemently for maintaining the offensive. A retreat into the gloomy Wilderness, they insisted, would negate all that had been accomplished over the past several days. But all offensive thoughts had left Hooker's mind, as he ordered his troops to concentrate and dig in near Chancellorsville. Darius N. Couch, leader of the Federal II Corps, bitterly concluded that "my commanding general was a whipped man."

Lee eagerly took the initiative. On the night of May 1, he and Jackson discussed how best to attack Hooker. The Federal left occupied strong ground and rested near the Rappahannock. A frontal assault against Chancellorsville would be too costly. The best course seemed to be turning the Union right, which ran west from Chancellorsville along the Orange Plank Road and Orange Turnpike (the two main east–west arteries through the Wilderness). Lee decided to divide his army again, sending Jackson's Second Corps on a flank march along narrow country roads. Lee would keep the 14,000 men of Richard H. Anderson's and Lafayette McLaws's divisions of Longstreet's corps to occupy Hooker's attention.

Jackson conducted the war's most celebrated flanking maneuver on May 2,

launching a powerful attack at about 5:15 PM that crushed Oliver O. Howard's Union XI Corps. Many of Howard's troops were Germans, and critics later accused the "damned Dutchmen" of fleeing without putting up a fight. In fact, no Union corps could have stood when Jackson's divisions swept out of the woods, shrieking the unnerving "Rebel Yell" and easily overlapping every potential defensive position. Half the regimental commanders and a quarter of the soldiers in Howard's corps fell during the fighting—evidence that they offered considerable resistance.

Darkness and confusion arising from the movement of large bodies of men through heavily wooded terrain slowed down the Confederate attack by about 7 PM. Jackson hoped to reform and renew the attacks later that night. Riding to the front with the goal of finding a way to cut Hooker off from the Rappahannock fords, he rode into the path

Few incidents in the war exceeded in boldness Lee's decision to send Jackson's corps on a flanking march around Hooker's right. One of Jackson's staff officers described the scene on the night of May 1 when the two generals plotted their strategy (depicted in this painting). "I found him [Jackson] seated on a cracker box with his back against a tree while opposite to him Gen. Lee sat on another box with his back against a tree. They were engaged in conversation." (Osprey Publishing)

of a volley from a North Carolina regiment. Wounded in three places, he had his left arm amputated later that evening.

Despite Jackson's impressive attack, Lee's troops at Chancellorsville remained separated by Hooker's much larger force. Extremely hard fighting on the morning of May 3 enabled the Confederates to reunite their wings at Chancellorsville and push

Oliver Otis Howard, a flag tucked under the stump of his right arm (he lost the limb at the Battle of Seven Pines), tries to rally his corps in the face of Jackson's flank attack. Having ignored warnings of an impending rebel attack, Howard exhibited courage on the field. He readily conceded that his lines collapsed "more quickly than it could be told." Two months later, his corps would be driven from the field again during the first day's fighting at Gettysburg. (Osprey Publishing)

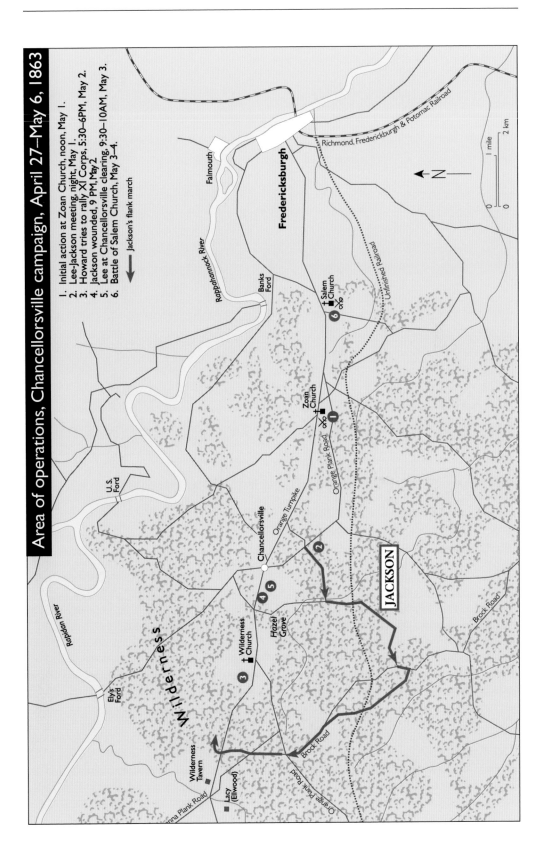

Area of operations, Chancellorsville campaign, April 27–May 6, 1863

1. Initial action at Zoan Church, noon, May 1.
2. Lee–Jackson meeting, night, May 1.
3. Howard tries to rally XI Corps, 5:30–6PM, May 2.
4. Jackson wounded, 9 PM, May 2.
5. Lee at Chancellorsville clearing, 9:30–10AM, May 3.
6. Battle of Salem Church, May 3–4.

→ Jackson's flank march

Richmond, Frederickburgh & Potomac Railroad

Falmouth

Fredericksburgh

Rappahannock River

Banks Ford

Salem Church

Unfinished Railroad

Zoan Church

U.S. Ford

Orange Plank Road

Chancellorsville

Orange Turnpike

Rapidan River

Wilderness

Wilderness Church

Hazel Grove

JACKSON

Brock Road

Ely's Ford

Wilderness Tavern

Lacy (Ellwood)

Orange Plank Road

N

0   1 mile

0   2 km

Hooker, who had been stunned when a southern artillery shell struck a pillar against which he was leaning, back closer to the Rappahannock. While a groggy Hooker sought to form a new defensive line, Lee guided Traveller, his sturdy gray warhorse, through thousands of Confederate infantrymen in a clearing near Chancellorsville. Emotions flowed freely as the soldiers, nearly 9,000 of whose comrades had fallen in the morning's fighting, shouted their devotion. Lee acknowledged their cheers by removing his hat. Seldom has the bond between a successful commander and his troops achieved more dramatic display. Colonel Charles Marshall of Lee's staff later wrote that Lee basked in "the full realization of all that soldiers dream of—triumph," adding: "As I looked upon him in the complete fruition of the success which his genius, courage, and confidence in his army had won, I thought that it must have been

Stonewall Jackson in front of the Confederate battle lines on the evening of May 2, 1863, just before being wounded by a volley from his own soldiers. This post-war engraving by Confederate veteran Allen C. Redwood mistakenly shows Jackson on the Plank Road. The General and his small party were on the Mountain Road, a smaller track that paralleled the Plank Road a few dozen yards to the north. (Author's collection)

from such a scene that men in ancient days rose to the dignity of gods."

Within minutes Lee learned that Sedgwick had broken Early's line at Fredericksburg and was moving towards Chancellorsville. He divided his army for a third time, deploying about half his troops to block this new threat. A sharp action on May 4 at Salem Church, located some 4 miles (6.4 km) west of Fredericksburg, stopped Sedgwick. That night Hooker decided to retreat, and by the morning of the 6th the Army of the Potomac had returned to the left bank of the Rappahannock.

Chancellorsville marked the apogee of Lee's career as a soldier and cemented the reciprocal trust between him and his men that made the Army of Northern Virginia so formidable. That trust radiated outwards to civilians in the Confederacy, who looked to Lee and his soldiers as their primary national rallying point from late 1862 onwards. Jefferson Davis gratefully thanked Lee "in the name of the people ... for this addition to the unprecedented series of great victories which your army has achieved." The success had come at terrible cost. Among the 12,674 Confederate casualties was Stonewall Jackson, whose death on 10 May cast a pall over the Confederacy. Lee would never find an adequate replacement for the gifted lieutenant whom he called his "right arm."

On the Union side, Chancellorsville dealt a telling blow to hopes for victory. Once again a northern army superior in numbers and equipment had suffered agonizing defeat. Once again a Federal commander had failed to commit all his troops to battle (two of the Union corps had lost fewer than 1,000 men). The northern butcher's bill

totalled 17,287. News of the defeat rocked Lincoln, who, while pacing back and forth, moaned, "My God! My God! What will the country say? What will the country say?" *New York Tribune* editor Horace Greeley rendered a common verdict: "It is horrible— horrible; and to think of it, 130,000 magnificent soldiers so cut to pieces by less than 60,000 half-starved ragamuffins!"

Chancellorsville exacerbated deep divisions in the North. A recently passed National Conscription Act, Lincoln's final Emancipation Proclamation (which took effect on January 1, 1863) and other issues fueled acrimonious debate. Hooker's failure increased unhappiness among northerners already disposed to criticize the Lincoln administration's conduct of the war. Even loyal Republicans wondered whether the rebels could be suppressed.

Lee at the Chancellorsville clearing on the morning of May 3, where he and his soldiers experienced an epiphany. The men believed victory would come whenever he led them, and he believed they could do whatever he asked. In this post-war engraving, Alfred R. Waud chose to place Lee on a dark horse rather than on the "Confederate gray" Traveller. (Author's collection)

Federals and Confederates in camp and in battle

Three million men served in the Union and Confederate armies, the majority of whom enlisted during the first two years of the war. They hailed from widely disparate backgrounds. Muster rolls reveal more than 100 pre-war occupations for Confederate soldiers and more than 300 for their northern counterparts. The 19th Virginia Infantry, for example, counted among its original members 302 farmers, 80 laborers, 56 machinists, 24 students, 14 teachers, ten lawyers, three blacksmiths, two artists, a distiller, a well-digger, a janitor, a dentist, and a quartet of men who identified themselves as gentlemen (the entire roster of occupations is too long to enumerate). Most northern regiments would have been even more diverse, though about half of the North's volunteers were farmers.

The typical soldier on each side was unmarried, white, native born, Protestant and between 18 and 24 years old. But many men younger then 18 served (some 10–14-year-olds as drummer boys or in other capacities), as did thousands of men in their thirties and forties (a few volunteered in their fifties, sixties and even seventies). First- or second-generation immigrants, mostly Germans or Irish, accounted for about one-quarter of the Union's soldiers. Foreign-born men made up just 9 percent of the Confederate forces. Although more than 175,000 black soldiers served in the Union armies before the end of the war, virtually none fought in the Eastern Theater between First Manassas and the Chancellorsville campaign.

It is difficult to generalize about what motivated such a large body of men to enlist and fight. Ideology certainly played a major role. Federals and Confederates used many of the same words to explain their actions, though the words could have different meanings. Many Union men spoke of liberty and the republican ideals for which the Revolutionary War generation had waged its struggle for independence. "Our Fathers made this country," an Ohio soldier remarked, "we, their children are to save it. … Without Union & peace our freedom is worthless." Untold other northerners fought to defend the sanctity of a Union they saw as a priceless democratic example. "I do feel that the liberty of the world is placed in our hands to defend," averred a Massachusetts private in 1862, "and if we are overcome then farewell to freedom."

Confederates also mentioned their Revolutionary forebears, as when a North Carolinian urged his father to "compare our situation and cause to those of our illustrious ancestors who achieved the liberties we have ever enjoyed and for which we are now contending." Thousands of southern soldiers, whether slaveholders or yeomen farmers, battled to defend their homes and the right to order their society as they saw fit. Just before the Battle of Chancellorsville, a member of the 44th Virginia Infantry described the conflict as "a struggle between Liberty on one side, and Tyranny on the other" and vowed to uphold the "holy cause of Southern freedom."

Beyond ideology or patriotism, men joined the army out of boredom or because of peer or community pressure. Others undoubtedly sought to participate in what they viewed as a great adventure or to pursue military glory that would impress their family and neighbours. From the outset, some white volunteers in the North saw the war as a crusade against slavery. The desire to maintain a robust masculine identity also figured in decisions to enlist. Mid-nineteenth-century American culture taught that it was a man's responsibility to his nation and family

The flag of the 2nd Wisconsin Infantry, a regiment in the Army of the Potomac's Iron Brigade. As part of the most renowned brigade in the North's largest army, the 2nd Wisconsin forged a record of splendid service. Nearly 20 percent of the men who served in its ranks were killed or died of wounds—the highest rate among all Union regiments. (Osprey Publishing)

to fight. More than one of these factors probably influenced most of the men.

The new soldiers marched off to war under banners charged with meaning. Often sewn by women in their community and presented at a public ceremony, the regimental flag later served as a reminder of the tie between men in the ranks and those at home. Flags also stood as the most obvious symbols of allegiance to a cause, evoking images of nation and state as well as community. Because loss of a flag in battle brought disgrace to a unit, many soldiers went to extreme lengths to protect their colors. In the fight in Miller's cornfield at the Battle of Antietam, for example, a veteran of the Texas Brigade recorded: "As one flag-bearer [in the 1st Texas Infantry] would fall, another would seize the flag, until nine men had fallen beneath the colors."

Once in the service, volunteers confronted a strange new world. Few had previously traveled far from home. Most had an ingrained, democratic aversion to hierarchy and bridled at military discipline (especially when the officers giving orders had frequently been acquaintances in their local communities). In June 1862, one exasperated soldier vowed that "When this war is over I will whip the man that says 'fall in' to me." Early in the conflict, enlisted men often elected the lieutenants and captains in their company and sometimes even their regimental colonels, lieutenant-colonels and majors. A Mississippian matter-of-factly described such an election in June 1861: "Held an election for field officers. W. S.

The flag of the 1st Texas Infantry, a regiment in the Army of Northern Virginia's famed Texas Brigade. The 1st Texas fought with distinction at Seven Pines, Gaines's Mill, Second Manassas, and, most famously, Antietam, where more than 80 percent of its men fell in fighting at the cornfield. (Osprey Publishing)

Featherston was elected [colonel] on the first ballot against Rodgers. Lyles was elected on the second ballot for Major, against Foote & Kay. The election for Lieut.-Col. failed because no one of the candidates got a majority. There has [sic] been two ballots." Popularity often trumped military skill among these candidates, which prompted virtually all professional soldiers to declare the elections pernicious.

Soldiers spent most of their days in camp. Tents provided shelter during the warmer months; huts in winter quarters. During the winter of 1862–63, a Union soldier described a typical hut: "Three of us have, by digging

Allen C. Redwood's engraving shows a ragged Confederate soldier eating an ear of corn during the 1862 Maryland campaign. A civilian who visited the battlefield at Antietam spoke bluntly about the physical effects of such a diet: "We traced the position in which a rebel brigade had stood or bivouaced in line of battle for half a mile by the thickly strewn belt of green corn husks and cobs, and also, *sit venia loquendi*, by a ribbon of dysenteric stools just behind." (Author's collection)

about 4 feet into the ground and raising it 6 logs high, then using our shelter tent for roofing, made quite comfortable quarters." Drill took up a vast amount of time and provoked wrathful complaints. In their free moments, the men wrote letters, read (newspapers and the Bible were favorite texts), played cards, indulged in various forms of gambling, and sometimes sought the company of prostitutes (venereal disease was a major problem in both armies). Pious men attended services conducted by chaplains and met in small prayer groups. Those less religiously inclined revelled in their freedom from old restraints. Shocked by the number of transgressions he detected among his comrades, one Virginian inelegantly described "some of the ornerest [orneriest: most stubborn] men here that I ever saw and the most swearing and card playing and fitin [fighting] and drunkenness that I ever saw at any place." A Federal put it more succinctly: "In our camps wickedness prevails to an almost unlimited extent."

Soldiers in both armies loved to sing. Each side had its patriotic songs, including "Dixie" and "The Bonnie Blue Flag" among Confederate favorites and "The Battle Hymn of the Republic" and "Yankee Doodle" as northern standards. Sentimental tunes exerted a powerful attraction for lonely men far from loved ones. Few songs enjoyed the popularity of "Home, Sweet Home," which appealed equally to men in both armies. The sound of hymns such as "Amazing Grace," "Rock of Ages," and "How Firm a Foundation" also floated above many a Civil War camp.

Food probably ranked first among a soldier's concerns. A member of the Army of the Potomac's Iron Brigade explained to his mother in January 1863 that "a good soldier cares more for a good meal than for all the glory he can put in [a] bushel basket." Union soldiers tended to be somewhat better fed than their Confederate counterparts. Staples of Union rations included beef or pork (salted or freshly dressed), coffee and tea, sugar, and, quite frequently, some type of vegetables. The northern bread ration was hardtack, which one veteran accurately described as "about the same size as common soda crackers we buy at home and perhaps a little thicker and made of two ingredients only, viz. flour & water without salt, Saleratus [baking soda], or shortening, & baked as hard as a hot oven will bake them so you can imagine what kind of bread it is." Confederates received far more pork than beef, with cornbread as their staple bread.

Men on both sides complained bitterly about the quality and quantity of their rations. Foraging and packages of food from home helped supplement rations, but many men complained of hunger. Shortages proved especially vexing to armies on the march, as commissaries struggled to transport sufficient foodstuffs. The Army of Northern Virginia suffered acutely during the 1862 Maryland campaign. "We are hungry," wrote one of Lee's soldiers of his ordeal north of the Potomac, "for six days not a morsel of bread or meat had gone into our stomachs—and our menu consisted of apples and corn."

Disease claimed the lives of two soldiers for every one killed in combat. Working before the age of many important breakthroughs in treatment, physicians lacked the knowledge and medicines to help their patients. Measles, mumps, whooping cough and chicken pox ravaged units in the early months of the war. Men from isolated rural backgrounds lacked the immunities of urban dwellers and suffered most cruelly. Diarrhea and dysentery ran rampant throughout the war. Malnutrition, filthy camps (soldiers often went for weeks without bathing) and tainted water from streams and ponds contributed to a woeful medical picture. So did poorly designed and located latrines. Many soldiers, avoiding the "sinks" because of foul odors and poor drainage, relieved themselves near sleeping areas— with results described by a Virginian in 1862: "On rolling up my bed this morning I found I had been lying in—I won't say what— something though that didn't smell like milk and peaches."

Wounded soldiers confronted a range of problems. Often left on the field for hours (or even days), they were taken to makeshift hospitals where overworked surgeons sought to cope with overwhelming numbers of patients. The vast majority of wounds were inflicted by shoulder weapons, typically 58-caliber smoothbore or rifle muskets. Physicians could do almost nothing for men shot in the torso, concentrating instead on those struck in the limbs. Most field surgery consisted of amputations, and many veterans left graphic descriptions of the grisly results. Houses, churches, barns and other structures near large battles were converted into field hospitals. In early May 1863, wounded soldiers from the Battle of Chancellorsville poured into Salem Church. "The sight inside the building," wrote a Georgia soldier, "for horror, was, perhaps, never equalled within so limited a space, every available foot of space was crowded with wounded and bleeding soldiers. The floors, the benches, even the chancel and pulpit were all packed almost to suffocation with them. The amputated limbs were piled up in every corner almost as high as a man could reach; blood flowed in streams along aisles and out at the doors."

Soldiers confronted their ultimate trial on the battlefield. Reared with heroic images of combat as depicted in woodcuts and paintings, they were ill prepared for the reality of noise, smoke, confusion, dismemberment, and death. Many green troops feared cowardice above all else, certain that word of faintheartedness in the face of the enemy would reach home. Men described a range of emotions and physical reactions as they braced for action. Some thought of loved ones; others experienced a surge of hatred towards their foe. Mouths grew dry, hearts pounded, arms and legs felt weak. Some men confessed to losing control of their bowels or involuntarily urinating. Most stood the test, though a good number inevitably ran or sought shelter.

Battle and its grisly aftermath set soldiers apart from civilians. During the Seven Days battles, a Texan who participated in the Confederate attacks at Gaines's Mill wrote, "I never had a clear conception of the horrors of war untill that night and the [next] morning. On going round on that battlefield with a candle searching for my friends I could hear on all sides the dreadful groans of the wounded and their heart piercing cries for water and assistance. Friends and foes all together." The "awful scene" made him wish never to "see any more such in life" and left him "heartily sick of soldiering." Many veterans developed a callousness readily apparent in their comments about scenes that would have horrified them earlier in the war. After the Battle of Antietam, one unusually hardened Federal affirmed that he did not "mind the sight of dead men no more than if they was dead Hogs." Another Union soldier groping to describe the carnage at Antietam revealed the inability of veterans to explain something civilians could never grasp. "No tongue can tell," he wrote, "no mind conceive, no pen portray the horrible sights I witnessed this morning."

Although desertion rates exceeded 10 percent in both armies and every unit had its share of malingerers and cowards, most common soldiers served honorably. They adjusted to their world of boredom in camp and terror on the battlefield, of capricious disease and the possibility of agonizing wounds. They forged a record that did credit to them and illuminated the degree to which they saw the conflict as a contest over important issues.

Salem Church, showing damage to its brick exterior from the fighting at Chancellorsville. Apart from its use as a hospital in May 1863, this Baptist church, which served a congregation organized in the 1840s, had also welcomed refugees from the Battle of Fredericksburg. A woman who visited the church in mid-December 1862 saw "several hundred refugees," some of whom sought rest in "the cold, bare church." (Author's collection)

Robert Augustus Moore, a Confederate soldier

Robert Augustus Moore participated in most of the Virginia campaigns during the first two years of the war. Born into a prosperous farming family near Holly Springs, Mississippi, on July 2, 1838, he enlisted as a private in an infantry company called the Confederate Guards shortly after Fort Sumter fell. The Guards subsequently became Company G of the 17th Mississippi Infantry Regiment. Mustered into service at Holly Springs, the 17th spent the last part of May and early June 1861 in Corinth before moving on to Virginia. As part of brigades commanded by D. R. Jones, Nathan G. ("Shanks') Evans, and William Barksdale between June 1861 and May 1863, the 17th fought at First Manassas, Ball's Bluff, Seven Pines, the Seven Days, Second Manassas, Antietam, Fredericksburg and Chancellorsville. Moore kept a pocket diary throughout his Confederate service that sheds light on his motivation for fighting, his opinions about important issues and his experiences in camp, on the march, and in battle.

Like many common soldiers North and South, Moore expressed a strong religious faith. He frequently attended church, seemingly unconcerned with denomination and able to draw strength from a variety of messages from the pulpit. "This is Thanksgiving day all over the Southern Confederacy," he wrote on November 15, 1861. "Our Chaplain held services in camp this evening notwithstanding the inclemency of the weather. I think all should join in praise to Him who has been with us in every engagement we have had with the enemy." On a rainy Sunday in Fredericksburg in February 1863, he attended services twice. "The church is quite commodious," he noted approvingly, "& is always crowded to overflowing with attentive hearers." The next day he observed that "Our chaplain is now carrying on a protracted meeting. Everything bids fair for the outpouring of God's spirit." He later affirmed that he could "recommend the atoning blood of Christ to all. All seems bright to me. I hope to walk so as never to bring reproach on the cause of Christ."

Moore's piety did not prevent his indulging in small vices. In October 1861, he welcomed a windfall of 30 bottles of whiskey, recording that he and his fellow soldiers "had a fine time drinking it." He often mentioned incidents when soldiers imbibed too much. "Lieut. Jackson came in this evening very tipsy," he wrote on November 8, 1861. "Was sent out as Lieut. of the pickets. The provo marshall was also drunk." Unused to the cold weather in Virginia, he considered an occasional drink essential. "This being a rainy & cold day, we all received a little toddy," he complained on one occasion. "I think the drams are a little too small for the weather & that they do not come around often enough to one in camp."

Moore's early life in the Deep South had not prepared him for Virginia's winters. During his first summer in Virginia, he betrayed a slightly scornful attitude towards residents who complained about the heat. "The weather is very hot for this climate, the people here think extremely hot," he recorded, "but it is not near so warm as in Miss." Cold was another matter. "Bad weather for ill-clad Rebels," he wrote on December 5, 1862, adding that the "Rebels are shivering around their log fires as the Yanks would say." Two days later the weather had got worse, producing "as cold a day as I have ever felt in Va." After a brief warming trend during the next week (when the Battle of Fredericksburg was fought), the mercury plunged downwards again. "This has been one of the most disagreeable days that I have ever experienced in camp," groused Moore. "The wind has blown very cold from the North & one could

Private Robert Augustus Moore, who wrote his diary in three 5 x 3-inch (12.7 x 7.6 cm) leather-bound volumes. (Author's collection)

barely live for the smoke from burning green juice wood. Cold—cold, indeed."

Unlike soldiers who resented every moment spent on drill, Moore understood that such labor paid off in discipline on the battlefield. He lamented his regiment's shortage of trained officers early in the war. "Went out this evening on battalion drill," he wrote in June 1861, "made a very bad show, many of the companies need drill in the school of the soldiers & need some better officers." Leaders who lacked apparent zeal for the war angered Moore, who in November 1861 applauded when "Orders were read out this evening on dress parade informing officers that they could not resign & go home, or that their resignations would not be accepted unless recommended by the Surgeon. This, I think, is right as a great number are resigning for no other purpose than to get home." Shortly thereafter he grumbled that "the majority of the men of our Regt. are becoming very wild & contracting many bad habits."

Moore seems to have remained steadfastly in the ranks except when ill. In a typical pattern, contagious diseases swept through the 17th Mississippi during the war's first summer. Moore and many others in his company endured a bout with measles in June 1861 that sent them to hospitals in Culpeper. Although he recovered in time to fight at First Manassas, a fever landed him back in the hospital at the end of July. Other physical problems plagued Moore and his comrades in the 17th, including sore feet when on the move. On March 12, 1862, the regiment "marched but six miles" and had "a large number of lame men ... who had to be hauled. Nearly all complain of their feet. The Pike is bad marching as the rocks are so rough." Here as in many other campaigns, most notably Lee's invasion of Maryland in 1862, roads with crushed stone surfaces wreaked havoc on poorly shod or barefoot soldiers.

Old and new loyalties sometimes clashed in Moore's ruminations. On January 8, 1862, his thoughts turned to an earlier war when all Americans had celebrated Andrew Jackson's victory over the British in the Battle of New Orleans. "This is the anniversary of the Battle of New Orleans," he wrote somewhat wistfully, "but we are so situated that we cannot celebrate it. Think we will have others more closely connected with the present generation to celebrate in the future, yet we should never forget the immortal hero of New Orleans."

As a southerner and slaveholder, Jackson represented a thoroughly acceptable hero for Moore. Although he never specifically mentioned slavery in his diary, Moore obviously believed the institution formed an essential element of southern society. He often labeled all northerners abolitionists, as when he mentioned receiving troubling news from Mississippi in February 1862: "Have received a letter from home. The Abolitionists have committed many acts of vandalism." Earlier in the conflict, he lauded white southern women willing to sacrifice their sons for the Confederacy. "When such sentiments are felt & expressed by the

Soldiers of William Barksdale's Mississippi Brigade fire at Union pontoon bridge-builders on December 11, 1862. Moore recorded that the fighting began about 9 AM. The Union bombardment of Fredericksburg commenced shortly thereafter and continued until about 4.30 PM, "when we were forced to retire down the river bank but held [the] Yanks out of the city until 8.00 p.m. when we retired & left the city in the hands of the Abolitionists."

matrons and men of our country," he commented, "I should like to know how the Abolitionists of the North can expect to conquer the South."

Moore consistently demonstrated a strong allegiance to the nascent Confederate republic. On New Year's Day in 1862, he rejoiced at southern "success in driving from our soil the ruthless invader who is seeking to reduce us to abject slavery." He predicted that a year hence "the North will have been taught a lesson not to be forgotten. We have already achieved many brilliant victories. May this prove a happy year to our country and to all mankind." Later that winter he affirmed his belief that "after much hard fighting" Confederates would "succeed in establishing our independence." He voluntarily re-enlisted for three years in February 1862 (the Confederate Conscription Act passed shortly thereafter would have kept him in the army anyway), taking care to explain his motivation: "I joined after long consideration, believing that in that way I could best serve my country. It seems to be sacrificing much, but what should we not be willing to sacrifice, even life itself, for the liberty of our country." White southerners who betrayed the Confederacy understandably upset him. "Have some very discouraging news from our homes in Miss.," he noted in December 1862. "Some are buying up & selling cotton to the abolitionists. Hope none of my friends or relatives are falling off so badly."

The change of years from 1862 to 1863 put Moore in a mood to reflect on his nation's future. The Confederacy had passed an eventful year in 1862, believed Moore, during which the North, "by the strength of numbers," more than once seemed likely to overrun the South. But by "heroic endurance, hard fighting & the favor of a just God," Confederates had resisted "every attempt at subjugation." Although Moore hated war, which he called the "greatest curse that can befall a land," he determined to fight on to victory. "We trust for success for our cause in the God of Battles," he averred. "We have had evidences that He is on our side & I hope for more signal display of His power in our behalf."

Promoted to corporal in April 1863, Moore anticipated a new season of campaigning. He had first experienced combat at First Manassas. He had fought the Union engineers who laid the pontoon bridges at Fredericksburg on December 11, 1862, and later heard "the groans of the wounded" after the slaughter of Burnside's attackers below Marye's Heights. During the Chancellorsville campaign, he and the 17th Mississippi fought under Jubal Early, delaying John Sedgwick's Union column at Fredericksburg while Lee and Jackson confronted Joseph Hooker in the Wilderness. Word of Jackson's death hit Moore very hard. "We to-day received the sad intelligence of the death of Lieut. Gen. Jackson who expired at Guinea" Station at 3 1/4 o'clock P.M. yesterday," he wrote in his diary. "No words can describe the sorrow with which this intelligence will be received from the Potomac to the Rio Grande."

Yet Jackson's death did not undermine Moore's morale or that of his comrades. "The opinion seems to prevail with us that hostilities will be resumed with us in a few weeks," he wrote on May 12, 1863. "The army, as far as I have seen is in excellent spirits." Moore marched into Pennsylvania with the army in June 1863. Surviving the Battle of Gettysburg, he travelled to northern Georgia with James Longstreet's corps in September. By that time he had been promoted to lieutenant. He was killed in action at the Battle of Chickamauga on September 20, 1863, along with 11 other members of the 17th Mississippi Infantry.

Northern and Southern society adjust to the demands of war

Although armies and battles often dominated the headlines, the war also touched the lives of millions of people behind the lines. Those in the Confederacy generally experienced the conflict more directly. The armies campaigned almost exclusively on southern soil, disrupting the Confederate economy and social structure to a far greater degree than was the case in the North. Yet both societies coped with a range of changes and tensions as they prosecuted a war while also addressing day-to-day needs.

The northern home front

The northern economy proved fully capable of producing ample war-related materials and consumer goods. Farmers grew record crops of wheat in 1862 and 1863 despite the absence of about a third of the agricultural workforce. The wide-scale use of machinery, including reapers and mowers, and the labor of women and children allowed production to increase. One observer in 1863 noted a "great revolution which machinery is making in production." "At the present time," he continued, "so perfect is machinery that men seem to be of less necessity. ... We have seen, within the past few weeks, a stout matron whose sons are in the army, with her team cutting hay at seventy-five cents per acre, and she cut seven acres with ease in a day, riding leisurely upon her cutter." As it fed soldiers numbering in the hundreds of thousands, the North managed also to exceed pre-war exports of beef, pork, corn, and wheat. Much of this bounty went to Great Britain, which imported a significant percentage of its grain from the North.

The United States government became a major purchaser of manufactured products and food, collecting goods for distribution to men in the ranks on a scale that anticipated patterns in two twentieth-century world wars. Several industries used antebellum technological advances to meet increased demand. In response to military contracts, production of canned foods, including condensed milk, shot up. Clothing manufacturers employed workers using sewing machines to churn out ready-made garments in standard sizes, and shoe factories delivered the nation's first mass-produced footwear differentiating between right and left feet. Shoulder weapons and pistols emerged from the assembly lines at arms companies in New England and elsewhere. Military-related businesses understandably benefited most from the war. Union soldiers wore wool uniforms, which helped double woollen production. Cotton textile firms, in contrast, felt acutely the loss of southern cotton. Northern railroads doubled their traffic and improved their tracks, engines, and rolling stock.

Although the northern economy presented a generally bright appearance, darker elements marred the overall picture. Wages lagged behind inflation, and strikes broke out in a number of industries. Anthracite coal miners in Pennsylvania accused the Lincoln administration of colluding with owners to keep wages low and break workers' resistance in the name of maintaining production vital to the national interest. Middle-class women entered the nursing profession in large numbers for the first time and filled some secretarial and clerical positions previously reserved mainly for men, but poorer women fared less well. They held roughly a third of the manufacturing jobs (up from about a quarter in 1860, and concentrated, as before the war, in such industries as textiles and shoe-making), receiving wages that increased at less than half the rate of men's. In the garment industry, for example, the piece rate declined from 17.5 cents to 8 cents per shirt during the first three years of the conflict. Women on single-family farms often struggled to plant and harvest crops and look after animals in the absence of husbands away at war. The widow of a poor soldier—whether he had been a farmer on marginal land or a laborer—often found herself literally cast into the streets. In 1863, despite a robust overall economy, women accounted for more than two-thirds of Philadelphia's vagrants.

Profiteers and speculators inevitably emerged. *Harper's Monthly* noted the rise of speculation as early as July 1861, quoting an "eminent financier" who allegedly remarked that the "battle of Bull Run makes the fortune of every man in Wall street who is not a natural idiot." Most loyal citizens resented those who profited unduly from the national crisis. Poorer northerners voiced especially venomous complaints about new fortunes built without honest labor. About midway through the war, the *New York Herald*, which reached a less affluent and educated audience than most of the major New York papers, undoubtedly touched a responsive chord among its wide readership with an unrestrained attack on the "dash, parade and magnificence of the new Northern shoddy aristocracy." "They are shoddy brokers in Wall Street," insisted the paper, "or shoddy manufacturers of shoddy goods, or shoddy contractors for shoddy articles for a shoddy government. Six days in a week they are shoddy business men. On the seventh day they are shoddy Christians."

The North financed the war with loans, paper money and taxes. War bonds generated about two-thirds of the required revenues. Marketed to individuals as well as to institutions, the bonds yoked people to the war effort and set a precedent that the great bond drives of the First and Second World Wars would emulate. In response to a shortage of hard money in the spring of 1862, Congress passed the Legal Tender Act, which authorized issuance of $150 million in Treasury notes (nearly $457 million of these "greenbacks" were eventually printed). Made

legal tender and printed at a time when Union armies seemed about to win the war, this paper money held its value well. Taxes accounted for roughly a fifth of Union revenues and included an income tax of 3–10 percent as well as various excise taxes. Without government-imposed rationing or price controls, inflation peaked at about 80 percent (in the Second World War, with controls, it reached 72 percent). The northern economy proved fully up to the task of producing guns and butter for the Union armies and northern civilians.

Political battles during the first half of the war revealed deep divisions in the northern populace. Much of the disagreement focused on war aims and emancipation. Within the Republican Party, the radicals argued from the outset that freedom for slaves should stand alongside restoration of the Union as a major goal. Hoping to appease slaveholding Border States and attract the broadest possible support from Democrats, Lincoln and other moderate Republicans preferred to keep Union paramount. Democrats almost universally hated the idea of forcing emancipation on slaveholders, insisting that they would fight for the Union but not for black freedom.

As the war unfolded in 1861 and 1862, the Republican-controlled Congress ended slavery in the federal territories and the District of Columbia, declared slaves owned by Confederates subject to confiscation, and guaranteed the freedom of thousands of slaves who had escaped to areas controlled by northern armies. By mid-July 1862, Lincoln had decided emancipation was necessary for northern victory, but he held off issuing a preliminary proclamation until Lee's retreat from Antietam. His final proclamation of January 1, 1863 signalled to the world that Union victory would strike the shackles from all slaves in the Confederacy (the proclamation did not apply to the loyal Border States). Frederick Douglass, a frequent critic of Lincoln, approvingly commented that the proclamation would give "a new direction to the councils of the Cabinet, and to the conduct of the national arms."

An 1863 cartoon from *Harper's Weekly* shows a trio of Democrats, their heads atop the bodies of copperhead snakes, closing in to strike at a beleaguered female representation of the Union. (Author's collection)

Most northern Democrats railed against this apparent shift in war aims. Working-class northerners feared economic competition from freed black people, with no group more vocal in this regard than recent Irish immigrants. Democratic newspaper editors and politicians prophesied that various evils would follow Lincoln's proclamation. Thousands of soldiers bluntly stated their opposition to fighting for emancipation. "I don't want to fire another shot for the negroes," wrote a German-born artillerist, "and I wish all the abolitionists were in hell."

Unhappy with the course of the war, a sizable portion of the Democratic Party called for an armistice to be followed by peace negotiations. Called Copperheads by their opponents after the venomous copperhead snake, these Democrats used the Emancipation Proclamation, the Conscription Act passed in the spring of 1863, claims of other Republican transgressions against civil liberties, and the Federal military disasters at Fredericksburg and Chancellorsville to build formidable support. Growing war weariness and the drumbeat of opposition from Copperheads made the spring and early summer of 1863 one of the gravest periods of the war for Lincoln and his supporters.

Still, the absence of southern Democrats from Congress enabled the Republicans to pass much of their legislative agenda in 1862–63. The National Bank Act of February 1863 sought to replace a plethora of state banknotes with a national currency that would promote economic development. The Homestead Act, which carried through on the old Free Soil idea of making western land available to free white settlers, passed in 1862, as did the Land-Grant College Act, designed to foster practical education in the mechanical and agricultural arts. The Pacific Railroad Bill of July 1862 offered substantial government support for the construction of the first transcontinental railroad. With all of this legislation, Republicans sought to construct a modern capitalist colossus.

The southern home front

In many ways, the Confederate home front presented a stark contrast to the North. With its capital heavily invested in land and slaves and lacking a sophisticated financial infrastructure, the Confederacy struggled to meet the demands of a massive war. Like the North, it resorted to three options to pay for the conflict. Congress enacted a series of national taxes, beginning with a modest direct property tax in the summer of 1861 and eventually adding others on personal income, consumer goods and wholesalers'

News of the bread riots spread quickly to the North, where this cartoon conveyed a very negative impression of the women in Richmond. Many middle- and upper-class Confederates also commented dismissively about the rioters, among them a Richmonder who called them "a heterogeneous crowd of Dutch, Irish, and free negroes" bent on looting businesses at random. (Author's collection)

profits. As a group, these taxes yielded only about 5 percent of the government's needs. An array of bonds provided another 35 percent of revenues. Treasury notes accounted for the remaining 60 percent and, as with paper money during the American

Revolution, proved to be a disaster. Inflation began almost immediately and quickly grew worse. The northern blockade, loss of agricultural areas to advancing Union armies and disruption of the southern transportation network (due to military activity and the absence of an industrial base able to replace worn-out tracks, engines, and rolling stock) caused shortages of crucial goods. These shortages combined with ever-larger issues of paper money to fuel inflation.

A clerk in the Confederate War Department named John Beauchamp Jones kept a diary that charted increasing financial hardships. In November 1861, he noted that "dry goods have risen more than a hundred per cent. since spring, and rents and boarding are advancing in the same ration." Ten months later, "blankets, that used to sell for $6, are now $25 per pair; and sheets are selling for $15 per pair, which might have been had a year ago for $4." Wood cost $16 per cord and coal $9 per load, provoking Jones to ask rhetorically, "How can we live here, unless our salaries are increased?" By the end of March 1863, the prices for wood and coal had reached $30 and $20.50 respectively, meat had "almost disappeared from the market, and none but the opulent can afford to pay $3.50 per pound for butter."

Many Confederates attributed shortages and soaring prices to hoarding by ruthless speculators. A group of women took to the streets in Richmond on April 2, 1863, to protest against prices and scarcities, smashing windows and looting stores in a "bread riot." Jones called it "a frightful spectacle, and perhaps an ominous one, if the government does not remove some of the quartermasters who have contributed very much to bring about the evil of scarcity. I mean those who have allowed transportation to forestallers and extortioners." Another diarist, much disturbed by news of the riot, remarked: "I fear that the poor suffer very much; meal was selling to-day at $16 per bushel. It has been bought up by speculators. Oh that these hard-hearted creatures could be made to suffer! Strange that men with human

hearts can, in these dreadful times, thus grind the poor."

Working-class and poorer farming families suffered most. Real wages declined by nearly two-thirds from their late-antebellum levels. Soldiers earned only $11 per month (Congress increased the sum to $18 in 1864), which left them virtually powerless to respond to pleas from home for economic help. As in the North, wives on small farms assumed greater burdens—but they did so in the midst of far more pernicious inflation. Many Confederates coped with spiraling prices by adopting a barter system and simply doing without items previously taken for granted. In the spring of 1863, Congress levied a 10 percent tax-in-kind on corn, wheat, potatoes, fodder, and other agricultural products, provoking outraged complaints and hitting smaller farmers especially hard.

Although formal parties never developed in the Confederacy, the nation divided politically over issues relating to the central government's efforts to wage an expensive war. The Richmond government not only taxed its citizens (there had been no direct taxes on citizens of the United States for many years prior to 1861), but also impressed supplies in return for paper currency, imposed martial law in some areas and, most ominously for those who feared a strong central power, conscripted men into the army from the spring of 1862 onwards. Jefferson Davis and other Confederate nationalists argued for the need to mobilize manpower, food, and other resources by whatever means necessary. A vocal minority that included Vice-President Alexander H. Stephens disagreed, accusing Davis of trampling on sacred state and individual rights. The President became a lightning rod for sometimes intemperate criticism. An extreme example of anti-Davis vitriol written in 1863 called the President a "miserable, stupid, one-eyed dyspeptic, arrogant tyrant who ... boasts of the future grandeur of the country which he has ruined, the soil which he has made wet with the tears of widows and orphans and the land which he has bathed in the blood of a people once free, but now enslaved. Oh, let me see him damned and sunk into the lowest hell."

Unlike their northern counterparts, most black and white southerners saw at least some direct evidence of the war. The appearance of Union armies created two kinds of refugee. Thousands of slaves made their way from southern farms and plantations to northern lines. In late May 1861, General Benjamin F. Butler, who commanded a Union enclave at Fort Monroe at the tip of Virginia's peninsula, refused to return some fugitive slaves to their masters. Butler called them "contraband of war" and remarked that loss of their labor would hurt the Confederacy (several of the men had been constructing southern fortifications). The term "contrabands" for escaped slaves soon caught on.

Over the next two years, as Union armies campaigned across the Confederacy, thousands of slaves left southern farms and plantations. They did so at great risk and, for the first 15 months of the conflict, with no guarantee of freedom. Placed in camps and often assigned to menial jobs with the army, their presence behind Union lines helped force the government to define the status of contrabands. In March 1862, Congress forbade the return of fugitives to Confederate owners, and the Second Confiscation Act of July 1862 declared slaves of rebel masters free. Lincoln's Emancipation Proclamation extended freedom to all slaves in the Confederacy, regardless of the owner's loyalty.

Slaves who remained at home also experienced change. With so many white men away in the army and old routines otherwise disrupted by the war, the bonds of slavery loosened somewhat. There were no slave uprisings in the Confederacy, but both white and black southerners understood that some of the rules no longer applied. Typical was Fannie Christian of Nelson County, Virginia, who wrote to the Secretary of War in June 1862 about her difficulties in running a farm and supervising slaves (her husband had been the overseer on this farm, whose 60-year-old owner was bedridden). Returning from a brief walk with a neighbor,

The inability of many slaveholders to provide their slaves with sufficient food and clothing helped undermine white authority. In this woodcut, four Confederate women accompanied by two slaves make their way to a Union commissary to request rations. (Author's collection)

Few images give a better sense of the war's displacement of Confederate civilians than this photograph of a family of refugees, their belongings tied down in a wagon, preparing to leave their home. Some refugees lacked the time even to gather belongings before departing. (Library of Congress)

explained Christian, she found that "one of the negroes had gone in the house and pull[ed] off her shoes and star[t]ed up[stairs], what to do I can not say." "I could do nothing but tell her to go out," continued the woman: "I have no one to correct them when they do [wrong]." She hoped her husband could be discharged from the army to look after things at home. "Im just surrounded with a gang of negroes," she stated, "i'am afraid abbout to get a breath." A woman in Winchester expressed similar concerns about two months later, reporting "a very annoying affair" with a slave who "took offense at some imagined grievance, and took up her baby and walked off." The slave soon returned to work, but her mistress pronounced herself prepared "at any moment to find she has gone off in earnest."

White families fleeing from advancing Union armies represented the second type of southern refugee. Among the first Confederate refugees was Mrs Robert E. Lee, who left her ancestral home at Arlington in May 1861 never to return. Thousands of displaced people congregated in Richmond, helping swell the city's population from about 40,000 in 1860 to more than 100,000 during the war. A diarist from northern Virginia recorded thoughts about abandoning her home: "I cannot get over my disappointment—I am not to return home! ... It makes my blood boil when I remember that our private rooms, our chambers, our very sanctums, are thrown open to a ruthless soldiery."

Thousands of other Confederates lived in areas either occupied by Federal forces or subject to frequent incursions. A woman in Warrenton, Virginia, described the impact of a single Union foray in April 1862. A party of Federals "came down to [a friend's] house and took every thing in the way of eating from him, his sugar, meat, and corn. ... They went to Mr Hunton's near Broad Run and stole all his *horses, hay, and corn—turkeys chickens, meat*, and in fact all the man had to live on." This woman believed that residents of towns fared better than those in rural areas: "The country people suffer much more ..., for parties go out as foraging parties and plunder and steal all they can lay their hands on."

Armies left indelible marks on the southern landscape. Battles scarred the areas around Manassas Junction, Fredericksburg and Richmond, but armies did not have to fight to have a devastating impact.

A British visitor traveling through Virginia's Piedmont in June 1863 left a graphic description of a region that had seen no important military clashes. "The country is really magnificent," he wrote, "but as it has supported two large armies for two years, it is now completely cleaned out. It is almost uncultivated, and no animals are grazing where there used to be hundreds." Fences had disappeared, buildings had been burned and chimneys had been left as silent sentinels. "It is difficult to depict and impossible to exaggerate," this witness concluded, "the sufferings which this part of Virginia has undergone."

As in the North, Confederate women played a more prominent part in the workforce. They filled in for their husbands on farms, served as full-time or occasional nurses, wrapped cartridges in ordnance facilities, and signed bond certificates or performed other clerical duties for the government. Their labors could prove to be not only exhausting but also dangerous. In March 1863, an explosion in an ordnance lab on Brown's Island in Richmond injured 69 women, at least 34 of whom died.

Between the beginning of the war and early summer 1863, Confederate civilians adjusted to a society thrown into considerable disarray. They coped with more shortages and relatively higher prices than northern civilians, endured the uncertainty and fear that Union armies inspired, and sometimes faced the cruel choice of whether to become refugees. Black southerners similarly encountered war-related problems, as well as opportunities, that affected them and their families. In sum, the South knew war in ways that were typical of other times and other nations, but that generally spared the people of the North.

Judith Henry's modest house stood at the epicenter of the Battle of First Bull Run. The armies returned to Henry Hill the following summer, fighting over the same ground during the Federal withdrawal at Second Bull Run. In this photograph, which could have been duplicated in many parts of Virginia where civilian structures were destroyed in 1861–63, a man stands amid the crumbling chimney and bits of framing that remained of Henry's house. (Author's collection)

Elizabeth Herndon Maury on the Virginia home front

The war came early to Elizabeth Herndon Maury. Born into a leading Virginia family in 1835, she was the daughter of famous oceanographer Matthew Fontaine Maury, and his wife, Anne Hull Herndon. She married a cousin named William A. Maury, and the couple were living in Washington, DC, with their young daughter when war erupted in 1861. Like Mrs Robert E. Lee, Betty and Will Maury became refugees almost immediately. Their staunch southern sympathies and loyalty to Virginia dictated that they move south. Over the next two years, Maury spent most of her time with relatives and friends in Fredericksburg, Richmond, and other places between those two cities. A diary for the period June 1861 to March 1863 details her thoughts and movements and illuminates several facets of civilian life in the Confederacy.

Maury made no apologies for her support of Virginia's decision to secede. When a gentleman from New York voiced regret at her father's resignation from the United States navy, Betty immediately defended the action. "He speaks ... of Pa's resignation ... as if he were dead," she wrote on June 3, 1861. "I told him that I was proud of my father before, but I was a hundred times prouder of him now." Northerners had always honored her father "far more than those at the South, but he could not take sides against his own people, against his native State and against the right." Betty bore no good will towards Virginians who failed to support the Confederacy. Learning of Winfield Scott's decision to retire as General-in-Chief of the Union armies in November 1861, she penned a scathing reaction: "Lincoln and his Cabinet called upon the old humbug to express their regret and thank him for his services to his country and his adherence to the Union," she wrote. "The old crocodile

Elizabeth Herndon Maury, whose diary was published privately by her daughter in 1938. The edition ran to just 25 copies, making it one of the scarcest and most desirable Civil War diaries. (Collection of Fredericksburg and Spotsylvania National Military Park)

was effected to tears and wishes that he was able to assist in crushing the rebellion. And he is a Virginian."

The precipitate departure from Washington had left Betty without most of her possessions—a common experience for Confederate refugees. She had lived a comfortable life, and she missed her things. A sense of longing and unpredictability accompanied a diary entry written in Fredericksburg in the summer of 1861: "It is strange how one can become accustomed to almost any mode of life. Here we are now *almost* as happy as in our best days and we cannot look into the future of this world at all. Cannot form an idea as to where or in what condition we may be one month hence."

Maury paid considerable attention to the problems of inflation and shortages of goods. Less than five months into the war, she noted that "every thing in the South in the way of dry goods and groceries are very high and continue to increase in price." The cost of sugar, tea, and coffee had escalated significantly, though meat and vegetables remained more affordable. "We can do without tea and coffee," she remarked, "until we whip the Yankees." By early April 1862, "goods of every kind" had become scarce, a spool of cotton had increased threefold in price, butter was unobtainable, and many shops had closed. Maury claimed that she and other Confederates did not mind the hardship "if we can only whip the Yankees and conquer a peace." Two months later the Federal army had occupied Fredericksburg, and "Yankee citizens and Yankee Dutchmen" had "opened all the stores on Main street." This brought a confusion of currencies that must have been typical of Confederate areas controlled by Union forces: "A pair of boots are worth so much in specie, so much more in Yankee money, and double their real value in Virginia money."

Civilians on both sides avidly followed news from the military fronts, relying on newspapers, letters from family members or friends, and rumors to shape their understanding of events. Betty Maury often commented about campaigns, battles, and generals. "More good news!" she exclaimed on July 22, 1861, upon learning of the Confederate victory at First Manassas. "The battle yesterday was more extensive than we thought. It extended along our whole line. The enemy are routed and we are in hot pursuit. Thank God, thank God, I hope it is all true. What would I not give to hear that they are now on Arlington Heights." Her enthusiasm abated the next day when it became clear that the Confederates had not hounded their beaten foe to Washington: "Am disappointed that our troops only pursued the enemy to Centreville. I had hoped they were now in Arlington."

The dreary procession of southern defeats in the Western Theater during the first half of 1862 upset her, but failed to break her resolve. "The news from the West is disastrous," she observed in mid-February 1862. "The enemy have penetrated into North Alabama as far as Florence. The coils of the 'Great Anaconda' seem to be tightening around us. That is the name the Yankees have given their plan to crush us simultaneously from all points. God help us." The surrender of New Orleans in late April 1862 elicited a defiant response from Betty: "The enemy has advanced with mighty strides in the last few months, but hope is strong with us yet."

Stonewall Jackson's exploits in the Shenandoah valley and McClellan's retreat from Richmond after the Seven Days thrilled Maury. On April 23, 1862, she lamented the absence of a great Confederate commander, predicting that "If we succeed in this struggle it will be in spite of our Generals. The man for the times has not yet been developed." Jackson soon emerged as Betty's ideal type of leader. With reports of his final successes in the valley in hand, she proclaimed, "Jackson is doing great things. He has whipped three of the Yankee Generals on three successive days. … He is somewhere between Winchester and Staunton." She mistakenly credited Stonewall with playing a major role in Lee's victory over McClellan in the Seven Days battles. "This has been a most anxious and exciting week and even now I am afraid to boast of the great deeds that have been done, and the fields that have been won by our brave soldiers in the past ten days," she wrote on July 5. "Jackson came down from the valley with a portion of his forces and got in McClellan's rear. We commenced the attack on Wednesday at Mechanicsville and God has blessed us with a series of glorious victories since then."

Living in Fredericksburg placed Maury near Virginia's military frontier for much of 1862 and early 1863. She worried ceaselessly about whether Union soldiers would appear and if she would have to move again. She also fretted about the well-being of relatives in Confederate service, including her brother Richard Launcelot, an officer with the 24th Virginia Infantry who suffered a serious wound at Seven Pines. The arrival of Federal troops opposite Fredericksburg in April 1862 proved to be almost anticlimactic. "One can scarcely realize that the enemy are so near and that we are in their hands," wrote Maury. "Every thing is so quiet. The stores have been closed for the last three days and the streets are deserted except by the negroes." A Union band's playing "Yankee Doodle" and "The Star Spangled Banner" on the night of April 20 spurred thoughts of Betty's earlier loyalties. "The old tunes brought back recollections of the old love for them," she wrote. "It was a sad and painful feeling."

Part of the pain derived from Betty's loss of her privileged pre-war economic circumstances. As a member of the South's slaveholding class, she had wanted for little

and shouldered no burden of work. Her mother commented in March 1862 about missing "the old Union sometimes. We never felt any of the evils of it and the advantages of being an independent nation will not be felt in our life time." Betty reflected on her mother's statements in her diary entry for that day: "I know what the answer is—that it

Refugees from the Battle of Fredericksburg huddle around a fire in this 1865 painting by David English Henderson. Betty Maury undoubtedly knew many of the people who fled the city as Burnside's army massed across the Rappahannock river in late November 1862. Robert E. Lee helped some of the civilians leave their homes. "I was moving out the women & children all last night & today," he wrote to his wife on November 22. "It was a piteous sight." (Gettysburg National Military Park, National Park Service)

is very plain we should have felt the evils in a short time very severely—that we are fighting for the good of posterity, that we may prevent a servile war, etc." Having listed the usual arguments in favor of secession and founding a new slaveholding republic, she admitted to "being unpatriotic enough to feel a little selfish sometimes and regret our peace and comfort in the old Union."

Betty's antebellum society had rested on a system of slavery that underwent enormous change in the midst of war. White southerners lost a measure of control over their slaves as Union military forces drew near, and thousands of black people in Virginia fled to Union lines. In mid-March 1862, as rumors of Union advances swirled through Fredericksburg, Betty noted that "seventeen of Mr Mason's servants have run off. They stole all of cousin Nanny's dresses but three, and took both cloak and shawl. One party of them went off in a wagon and carried their feather beds."

In late April, after Federal troops had reached Fredericksburg, Maury wrote that the "negroes are going off in great numbers, and are beginning to be very independent and impudent. We hear that our three are going soon." The reality of war mocked the notion, so often trumpeted by white southerners, that slaves were happy with their lot. Indeed, the specter of slaves

wreaking vengeance on their old masters haunted Confederates such as Betty Maury. "I am afraid of the lawless Yankee soldiers," she wrote, "but that is nothing to my fear of the negroes if they should rise against us."

Maury had moved to Richmond by the time of the Battle of Fredericksburg. She celebrated Lee's victory over Burnside, but lamented the destruction of much of the city. In the neighborhood where she had lived, reports indicted that "almost every house has six or eight shells through it, the doors are wide open, the locks and windows broken and the shutters torn down." Two blocks of buildings had been burned, and "our house was a hospital."

Maury soon faced a more personal challenge. Pregnant with a second child in the spring of 1863, she learned that cousins from whom she rented rooms in Richmond meant to turn her out. "No one will be willing to take us," she wrote, "when told that I expect to be confined in a month or two. It is most unchristian and uncharitable treatment." An aunt in central Virginia declined to provide a place for Betty and her daughter, after which the pair endured a difficult trip to Charlottesville, where the new child was born on June 7. Betty Maury lived another 40 years, having experienced in full measure the traumatic events of the Civil War era.

An uncertain future

Two years of war in the Eastern Theater had not produced a decisive resolution on the battlefield. The armies had waged six major campaigns, testing each other's mettle twice on the plains of Manassas, in the fetid lowlands outside Richmond, amid the rolling Maryland countryside near Sharpsburg, on the banks of the Rappahannock river at Fredericksburg, and at Chancellorsville in the dreary thickets of the Wilderness. More than 150,000 men had fallen on these fields, mocking the widespread belief in 1861 that the conflict would be settled on a single battlefield. Dramatic fluctuations of military fortunes had taught perceptive observers not to expect Cannae-type victories.

Most people North and South, weary of the war's butchery and general disruption of normal patterns of life, hoped for peace but saw no end in sight. Voicing a sentiment prevalent in both armies, one of Lee's soldiers wrote after Chancellorsville: "I have never felt as tired of the army since I have been in it as I am now. ... I'm hoping for a time when the filth, lice, scurvy, and slavery of war shall be a thing of the past—and then—I close my eyes and am off to the dim and dusky future peopling it with dreams which I know are too bright ever to be realized."

Only the South had succeeded in the search for competent military leadership. With Lee's emergence during the Seven Days, Confederates had found the general whose talent and achievements would place him at the center of their quest for nationhood. Stonewall Jackson had been Lee's peerless lieutenant, the pair forming a seemingly unbeatable team. Jackson's death plunged the Confederacy into mourning. "He was the nation's idol," wrote one woman, "not a breath even from a foe has ever been breathed against his fame. His very enemies reverenced him. God has taken him from us

that we may lean more upon *Him*, feel that He can raise up to himself instruments to work His Divine Will." An officer in the Army of Northern Virginia commented that "No man in the Confederacy would have been more missed and more deeply lamented, except Lee perhaps." Many who lamented Jackson's loss tried to put on a brave face, as when Richmond's diarist J. B. Jones wrote that "there are other Jacksons in the army, who will win victories—no one doubts it."

Although most Confederates looked with confidence to Lee and his army, they harbored few illusions about how quickly the war would end. A Richmond paper observed in mid-May 1863 that the "Yankees have now made up their minds that this is to be a long war, and they are determined to fight it out to the end. Of course, we shall beat them in every battle, but they can afford to lose five men for the sake of destroying *one* of us." The paper grimly concluded that the Confederates fought "at fearful disadvantage with terrible loss, in spite of our superiority in pluck and in generalship, and the state of things may well continue twenty years longer, for these mean Yankees cannot afford to acknowledge our independence."

The Army of the Potomac's high command had endured enormous turmoil during two years of fighting, and few in the North believed in Joseph Hooker. A staff officer in the VI Corps captured the frustration of several failed campaigns in a single sentence: "I hope we shall not have to cross this river again," he wrote from camp near the Rappahannock on May 12, 1863, "for it is not the way to Richmond but I am afraid we shall have to try it over again and that very soon." Elizabeth Blair Lee, whose husband Samuel Phillips Lee served as a Union admiral, took heart from rumors that

George G. Meade, John Sedgwick, and other subordinates had told Hooker they "would never willingly go in battle under him again." Although Lee's information was faulty, her sentiment underscored the lack of trust in Hooker.

The North could take heart from the fact that Great Britain and France had backed away from recognizing the Confederacy. In mid-September 1862, with Lee's victories at the Seven Days and Second Manassas in mind, Prime Minister Viscount Palmerston and Foreign Secretary Lord John Russell had concluded that the Confederacy was winning the war. If Lee triumphed again while in Maryland, suggested Palmerston, Britain and France should offer "an arrangement upon the basis of separation" between the United States and the Confederacy.

The Union soldiers who fought at Antietam helped change the picture radically. Following Lee's retreat and Lincoln's issuance of the preliminary proclamation of emancipation, Palmerston decided that the "whole matter is full of difficulty, and can only be cleared up by some more decided events between the contending armies." In late October, the British Cabinet rejected a French proposal for a six-month armistice and suspension of the Union blockade. Because emancipation had been added to the northern agenda, it would take a spectacular series of Confederate victories to bring European intervention.

Each side girded for another round of campaigning in late spring 1863. During the lull after Chancellorsville, events in the Western Theater contended for primacy. "Affairs in the South West now engage all our attention," stated Catherine Edmondston on May 23. For two years, Union forces had fought to gain control of the Mississippi river, and the Confederacy retained just two bastions on that mighty waterway—at Vicksburg, Mississippi, and Port Hudson, Louisiana. But whatever happened west of the Appalachians and along the Mississippi, no one doubted that future confrontations between the Army of the Potomac and the Army of Northern Virginia would do much to shape the destinies of the two North American republics.

Glossary

casualty A life that is lost as a result of war or some other type of conflict.

Civil War The American battle from 1861–1865 between the Northern and Southern states for the fate of the Union. Generally, the term refers to a war between factions within a nation.

confederate A term that describes affiliation with the Southern states during the Civil War.

Constitution The United States doctrine that was signed in 1787, which acts as the supreme law of the nation.

Emancipation Proclamation The executive orders issued by President Abraham Lincoln during the Civil War that effectively ended slavery in ten states.

inflation The economic phenomenon of too much money chasing too few goods, resulting in rising prices and weakening buying power of currency.

infrastructure The inner public works of a country, such as roads, schools and public buildings.

North The designation given to the northern states that were part of the Union during the Civil War.

ration To distribute in degrees in order to save for the long term.

secession The act of a group or organization breaking affiliation with another group or organization.

slavery The act of making a person work by threat of force.

South The designation given to the southern states that were part of the Confederacy during the Civil War.

sovereignty During the Civil War, having freedom from federal governmental rule.

theater Relating to war, the broad area where a group of battles are fought.

union The political group during the Civil War that allied with the Northern states.

West Point The famous military academy established in 1802 in West Point, New York.

For more information

American Civil War Society
21910 Germain Street
Chatsworth, CA 91311
(805) 497-7020
Web site: http://www.acws.net
The American Civil War Society is based in Southern California and has a membership of 800 people. It hosts a variety of Civil War reenactments.

Civil War Antiques Preservation Society
1085 Commonwealth Avenue, Suite 410
Boston, MA 02215
(410) 750-3502
Web site: http://www. civilwarpreservation.com
The mission of the Civil War Antiques Preservation Society is to commemorate and keep artifacts from the Civil

War era that offer historical and intellectual value.

Civil War Education Association

P. O. Box 78
Winchester, VA 22604
(800) 298-1861
Web site: http://www.cwea.net
An organization dedicated to presenting Civil War tours, seminars and symposiums to foster an understanding of this revolutionary era in American history.

Civil War Preservation Trust

1156 15th Street NW, Suite 900
Washington, DC 20005
(202) 367-1861
Web site: http://www.civilwar.org
The Civil War Preservation Trust is an organization who's mission is to preserve the lands that were directly involved in the Civil War.

Lincoln Group of New York

P.O. Box 220
Newton, NJ 07860
Web site: http://www.lincolngroupny.org
The Lincoln Group of New York is dedicated to the study of the life of Abraham Lincoln.

National Civil War Association

P.O. Box 151
Santa Clara, CA 95052-0151
(800) 662-1863
Web site: http://www.ncwa.org
The National Civil War Association (NCWA) is designed to educate the public about the Civil War.

Philadelphia Society

11620 Rutan Circle
Jerome, MI 49249
(225) 927-2042
Web site: http://www.phillysoc.org
The Philadelphia Society was established in 1964 and its mission is "to sponsor the interchange of ideas through discussion and writing, in the interest of deepening the intellectual foundation of a free and ordered society."

Web sites

Due to the changing nature of Internet links, Rosen Publishing has developed an online list of Web sites related to the subject of this book. This site is updated regularly. Please use this link to access the list:

http://www.rosenlinks.com/cweh/easta

For further reading

Bearss, Edwin C. *Fields of Honor: Pivotal Battles of the Civil War.* New York, NY: National Geographic, 2007.

Goodwin, Doris Kearns. *Team of Rivals: The Political Genius of Abraham Lincoln.* New York, NY: Simon & Schuster, 2006.

Hazen, Walter A. *Everyday Life: The Civil War* (Everyday Life). Tucson, AZ: Good Year Books, 2007.

Hyslop, Steve. *Atlas of the Civil War: A Complete Guide to the Tactics and Terrain of Battle.* New York, NY: National Geographic, 2009.

Hyslop, Steve. *Eyewitness to the Civil War.* New York, NY: National Geographic, 2006.

Johnson, Jennifer. *Gettysburg: The Bloodiest Battle of the Civil War.* New York, NY: Franklin Watts, 2009.

Judson, Clara Ingram. *Abraham Lincoln: Friend of the People.* New York, NY: Sterling Point Books, 2007.

Keegan, John. *The American Civil War: A Military History.* New York, NY: Knopf, 2009.

Magoon, Kekla. *Abraham Lincoln* (Essential Lives). Edina, MN: Abdo Publishing Company, 2007.

Mattern, Joanne. *The Big Book of the Civil War: Fascinating Facts About the Civil War, Including Historic Photographs, Maps, and Documents.* New York, NY: Running Press, 2007.

McNeese, Tim. *Civil War Battles* (The Civil War: a Nation Divided). New York, NY: Chelsea House, 2009.

McPherson, James M. *Abraham Lincoln.* New York, NY: Oxford University Press, 2009.

McPherson, James M. *Tried by War: Abraham Lincoln as Commander in Chief.* New York, NY: Penguin, 2009.

Mountjoy, Shane. *Causes of the Civil War: The Differences Between the North and South* (The Civil War: a Nation Divided). New York, NY: Chelsea House, 2009.

Parker, Christi E. *Civil War Is Coming: Expanding & Preserving the Union* (Primary Source Readers). Huntington Beach, CA: Teacher Created Materials, 2008.

Reis, Ronald A. *African Americans and the Civil War* (The Civil War: a Nation Divided). New York, NY: Chelsea House, 2009.

Silvey, Anita. *I'll Pass for Your Comrade: Women Soldiers in the Civil War.* New York, NY: Clarion Books, 2008.

Swanson, James L. *Manhunt: The 12-Day Chase for Lincoln's Killer.* New York, NY: Harper Perennial, 2007.

Bibliography

I. Primary sources

Alexander, E. P., *Fighting for the Confederacy,* Chapel Hill, NC, 1989.

Berlin, I., and others (eds), *Free at Last: A Documentary History of Slavery, Freedom, and the Civil War,* New York, 1992.

Delbanco, A. (ed.), *The Portable Abraham Lincoln,* New York, 1993.

Edmondston, C. A. D., *Journal of a Secesh Lady,* Raleigh, NC, 1979.

Lee, R. E., *The Wartime Papers of R. E. Lee,* Boston, MA, 1961.

McClellan, G. B., *The Civil War Papers of George B. McClellan,* New York, 1989.

Miers, E. S. (ed.), *A Rebel War Clerk's Diary,* Baton Rouge, LA, 1993.

Nevins, A., *Diary of George Templeton Strong,* 4 vols, New York, 1952.

II. Secondary sources

Catton, B., *Glory Road,* Garden City, NY, 1952.

Cooper, W. J., *Mr Lincoln's Army,* Garden City, NY, 1951.

Cooper, W. J., *The South and the Politics of Slavery, 1828–1856,* Baton Rouge, LA, 1978.

Crook, D. P., *The North, the South, and the Powers: 1861–1865,* New York, 1974.

Curry, L. P., *Blueprint for Modern America: Nonmilitary Legislation of the First Civil War Congress,* Nashville, TN, 1968.

Davis, W. C., *Battle at Bull Run,* Garden City, NY, 1977.

Davis, W. C., *"A Government of Our Own": The Making of the Confederacy,* New York, 1994.

Donald, D. H., *Lincoln,* New York, 1995.

Freeman, D. S., *Lee's Lieutenants: A Study in Command,* 3 vols, New York, 1942–45.

Gallagher, G. W. (ed.), *The Fredericksburg Campaign: Decision on the Rappahannock*, Chapel Hill, NC, 1995.

Gallagher, G. W. (ed.), *Chancellorsville: The Battle and Its Aftermath*, Chapel Hill, NC, 1996.

Gallagher, G. W., *The Confederate War*, Cambridge, MA, 1997.

Gallagher, G. W. (ed.), *The Antietam Campaign*, Chapel Hill, NC, 1999.

Hattaway, H., and Jones, A., *How the North Won: A Military History of the Civil War*, Urbana, IL, 1983.

Hennessy, J. J., *Return to Bull Run: The Campaign and Battle of Second Manassas*, New York, 1993.

Jones, H., *Union in Peril: The Crisis over British Intervention in the Civil War*, Chapel Hill, NC, 1992.

Klatcher, P., *Flags of the American Civil War 3: State and Volunteer*, Oxford,

Klement, F. L., *The Limits of Dissent: Clement L. Vallandigham and the Civil War*, Lexington, MA, 1970.

Massey, M. E., *Bonnet Brigades: American Women and the Civil War*, New York, 1966.

Massey, M. E., *Refugee Life in the Confederacy*, Baton Rouge, LA, 1964.

McPherson, J. M., *Battle Cry of Freedom: The Civil War Era*, New York, 1988.

McPherson, J. M., *For Cause and Comrades: Why Men Fought in the Civil War*, New York, 1997.

Mitchell, R., *Civil War Soldiers*, New York, 1988.

Paludan, P. S., *"A People's Contest': The Union and the Civil War, 1861–1865*, New York, 1988.

Potter, D. M., *The Impending Crisis, 1848–1861*, New York, 1976.

Rable, G., *The Confederate Republic: A Revolution Against Politics*, Chapel Hill, NC, 1994.

Sears, S. W., *Chancellorsville*, Boston, MA, 1996.

Sears, S. W., *Landscape Turned Red: The Battle of Antietam*, New York, 1983.

Sears, S. W., *To the Gates of Richmond: The Peninsula Campaign*, New York, 1992.

Silbey, J. H., *A Respectable Minority: The Democratic Party in the Civil War Era, 1860–1868*, New York, 1977.

Smith, C., *Chancellorsville 1863*, Oxford, 1998.

Smith, C., *Fredericksburg 1862*, Oxford, 1999.

Tanner, R. G., *Stonewall in the Valley: Thomas J. "Stonewall" Jackson's Shenandoah Valley Campaign, Spring 1862*, Mechanicsburg, 1996.

Thomas, E. M., *The Confederate Nation, 1861–1865*, New York, 1979.

Index

About the authors

Professor Robert O'Neill, AO D.Phil, is the Chichele Professor of the History of War at the University of Oxford and series editor of *Essential Histories*. His wealth of knowledge and expertise shapes the series content, and provides up-to-the-minute research and theory. Born in 1936 as an Australian citizen, he served in the Australian army from 1955 to 1968 and has held a number of eminent positions in history circles. He has been Chichele Professor of the History of War and a Fellow of All Souls College, Oxford, since 1987.

He is the author of many books including works on the German army and the Nazi party, and the Korean and Vietnam wars.

Gary W. Gallagher is the John L. Nau III Professor in the History of the American Civil War at the University of Virginia. He is the author of several books, among them *Lee and His in War and Memory*, *The Confederate War*, and *Stephen Dodson Ramseur: Lee's Gallant General*. He also serves as editor and co-author of the *Military Campaigns of the Civil War* series, which includes titles on seven operations.